A Handbook of Job Aids

Allison Rossett

and

Jeannette Gautier-Downes

JOSSEY-BASS/PFEIFFER
A Wiley Company
www.pfeiffer.com

Published by

JOSSEY-BASS/PFEIFFER
A Wiley Company
989 Market Street
San Francisco, CA 94103-1741
415.433.1740; Fax 415.433.0499
800.274.4434; Fax 800.569.0443

www.pfeiffer.com

Jossey-Bass/Pfeiffer is a registered trademark of John Wiley & Sons, Inc.

ISBN: 0-88390-290-7
Library of Congress Catalog Card Number 91-9090

Library of Congress Cataloging-in-Publication Data

Rossett, Allison

    A handbook of job aids/Allison Rossett and Jeannette Gautier-Downes.
      p.   cm.
    Includes index.
    ISBN 0-88390-290-7 (acid-free paper)
    1. Employees—Training of.   2. Visual aids.   3. Teaching—Aids and devices.   I. Gautier-Downes,
Jeannette.   II. Title.   III. Title: Job aids.
    HF5549.5.T7R647   1990
    658.3'12404—dc20

Printed in the United States of America

Printing   20 19 18 17 16 15 14 13 12 11

We at Jossey-Bass strive to use the most environmentally sensitive paper stocks available to us. Our publications are printed on acid-free recycled stock whenever possible, and our paper always meets or exceeds minimum GPO and EPA requirements.

Contents

Part 1: Understanding Job Aids

Part 2: Developing Job Aids

Part 3: Examples of Job Aids

Part 4: Trends in Job Aids

Dedication

This book is dedicated to
Sue, Catherine, Julie, Kristen, Raider, and Mandela.

Acknowledgments

So many people deserve our thanks. First, there are our many colleagues who have written and spoken about job aids and information. Although they are listed in the References sections of each chapter, we'd like to mention some of them here as well: Fritz Brecke, Clay Carr, Ruth Clark, C.S. Duncan, George Geis, Gloria Gery, Tom Gilbert, Joe Harless, Paul Harmon, Jeff Nelson, Marc Rosenberg, and Susan Zagorski.

Second, we want to acknowledge the people and organizations who shared their examples and thoughts with us. They are credited within chapters and are listed in the Credits section that follows. We want to express special thanks to these contributors. This book would suffer without the real-life instances and commentaries they generously provided.

Third, a thank you to graduate students at San Diego State University. They endured early versions of the chapters, contributed examples and suggestions, and are responsible at least in part for the end product.

Finally, our thanks go to friends and colleagues who read the chapters and provided advice. Thanks to Jeff Brechlin, Anne Derryberry, Mary Harris, Linda Paulsen, and Sue Reynolds. *A Handbook of Job Aids* would have been less useful and less readable without their efforts.

Credits

We wish to express appreciation to the following contributors and their organizations. Their works are included by permission.

Addison, Roger. (Figures 5.4 and 8.3). *Cost Justification Work Sheet.* Copyright © 1988, Wells Fargo Bank, Retail Staff Development, San Francisco, CA. Used for Branch Production Management.

Addison, Roger. (Figures 5.9 and 6.7). *Using and Selecting Contractors.* Copyright © 1988, Wells Fargo Bank, San Francisco, CA. For internal use.

Apple Computer, Inc. (Figures 11.1, 11.2, 11.3, and 11.4). Various HyperCard graphic illustrations © Apple Computer, Inc. Used with permission. HyperCard and HyperTalk are registered trademarks of Apple Computer, Inc., licensed to Claris Corporation.

Boothe, Barry. (Figure 8.1). (1989). *Heads.* Caterpillar, Inc., Joliet, IL.

Boucher, Richard. (Figure 5.16). *Manage I/O Ports.* Copyright © 1989, Prime Computer, Inc., Natick, MA. All Rights Reserved. The material on pages 72 and 73 is printed with the permission of Prime Computer, Inc., the copyright owner, copyright 1989, Prime Computer, Inc. All rights reserved. No portion of the material may be reproduced without the express written consent of Prime Computer, Inc.

Brown, Denise. (Figures 5.5 and 7.1). *Outgoing Federal Returns.* Sovran Bank, N.A., Richmond, VA.

Bruttig, Dana. (Figure 8.5). (1989). *Quick Reference to Prospecting.* Century 21 Real Estate Corporation, Irvine, CA. Provided courtesy of Century 21 Real Estate Corporation. All references are with the permission of Century 21 Real Estate Corporation, and all rights to this job aid have been reserved by Century 21 Real Estate Corporation.

Buzinski, Andy. (Figure 5.3). (1987). Worksheet for Pricing Training Proposals. *Performance and Instruction, 26*(6), 26.

Clark, R. (Figure 5.2). (1986). Defining the 'D' in ISD: Part 2: Task-specific instructional methods. *Performance and Instruction, 25*(3), 17.

Federal Income Tax (Rev. Nov. 88). (Figures 5.13, 5.14, and 5.15). Department of the Treasury, Internal Revenue Service.

Finnegan, Gregory. (Figure 7.3). (1990). *Port-A-Cath.* Robert Wood Johnson University Hospital.

General Telephone of California, Education and Training Department. (Figures 5.8 and 9.1). RC 2352A, RC 3252A, Monrovia, CA.

Hale, Judith A., and Westgaard, Odin. (Figure 5.7). *Parliamentary Process.* Hale Associates, Oak Brook, IL.

Harmon, Paul. (Figures 11.6 and 11.7). *Diagnostic Expert Systems for Instructional Designers.*

Hoffman, Marianne C. (Figure 9.2). (1989). *Manage Equipment Maintenance.* This job aid was developed by Marianne Hoffman while she was Head of Training Development, NMPC DET NRSU. It is in the public domain having been created by a United States Navy employee on Navy time.

Houck, Amara. (Figure 4.5). The bandanna illustrations were created especially for *Women's Outdoor Journal* by Amara Houck of Rockport, IN.

McKinnon, Diane. (Figure 7.4). (1989). *Default Programmable (PF) Key Settings for Mainframe Computer System.* Intel Corporation.

Mitchell, Andrea. (Figure 8.4). (1989). *Computing Per Diem.* The Mitchell Group, Silver Springs, MD.

Morse, Karen. (Figure 9.3). (1989). *Performance Management Checklist.* Sharp HealthCare, Management Development Department. Created by the members of the Management Development Department.

Pasigna, Aida L., and Thiagarajan, Sivasailam. (Figure 5.12). *A Checklist for Simplifying Your Language for Non-English Speakers.* Institute for International Research, Bloomington, IN.

Patterson, Patricia. (Figure 7.2). (1990). *ACG Networking Job Aid.* Alexander & Alexander Consulting Group, Inc.

Rossett, Allison. (Figure 5.10). (1987). *Training Needs Assessment.* Englewood Cliffs, NJ: Educational Technology Publications, pp. 219-220.

Ruch, Marcella. (Chapter 4, page 51). "Altering Your Home to Support Weight Loss."

Schulman, Michael J., and Mitchell, Donald, L. (Figures 5.1 and 8.2). *E.1 Turn on Machine and Access AMCISS Main Menu* and *E.6 Query Data.* Performance Engineering Network, Inc., Yorktown, VA. Developed for the Army Logistics Management College, Ft. Lee, VA, under contract to the Office of Personnel Management, Washington, D.C., by Performance Engineering Network, Inc., a venture partner of the Personnel Management Organization.

Shmikler, Sam. (Figure 9.4). (1989). *20 Things You Can Do Within 99 Seconds to Improve Your Negotiations*, The Pacific Group.

Wackerman, Joan. (Figure 4.2). *Instructor Guide Development Checklist.* Alexandria, VA.

Wagner-Davis, Steven. (Figure 4.6). *Interacting with Telecommunications Software.* San Diego, CA.

Wolfe, Michael. (Figure 4.7). *User Input-Machine Response.* San Diego, CA.

Zagorski, Susan. (Figure 6.4). (1987). How to open a jar of miso. *Performance and Instruction*, 28(10), 16.

Preface

This book was written because I finally heard what Tom Gilbert and Joe Harless had been saying for years. In books and speeches, for at least a decade, I had listened to their exhortations regarding the fruitful distinction between information and education. I had agreed with them, perfunctorily encouraged my students and clients to rely on the information supports that are commonly called job aids, and concentrated my attention on needs assessment and instructional design.

Then four things happened. First, I began to read about information. I read Warren Bennis, Saul Wurman, Donald Norman, Joe Harless, Peter Pipe, Clay Carr, William Davis, Allison McCormack, Shoshana Zuboff, John Naisbitt, Richard Rosenberg, and many others. I began to see the implications of enriching the environment with information versus storing data or perspectives in someone's memory.

The second thing that happened was a conscious decision to contribute to a paradigm shift in American and international organizations. In the past, training professionals were judged by how much training they offered. Now organizations and professionals are beginning to be judged by how much performance they support and by the systems they build that help people to work without costly training. We can hear the clarion calls for re-engineered work and just-in-time information and training support.

The third influence is new technologies. Taking organizations by storm, technological change will serve as both the reason and the vehicle for information support. I read Gloria Gery, Marc Rosenberg, and Jerry Puterbaugh, and I tinkered with on-line help, expert, and performance-support systems. They are the future of job aids, a future that is only beginning to be realized.

The fourth factor was my inability to find a print resource on job aids to which I could send graduate students and clients. Although fine workshops exist, there was not an affordable handbook about understanding, using, and developing job aids. People need a way of thinking about job aids that is congruent with contemporary theory, practice, and trends. And they need examples and more examples.

I asked Jeannette Gautier-Downes, an experienced job-aid developer, to join me to make certain that we would have many and varied examples and commentaries from developers. She knew what practitioners needed and represented that perspective. I worked hard to find a way of conceptualizing job aids that ensures appropriate and expanded ways of using them.

This handbook is for two types of users. The first is the individual who wants to begin understanding and providing information supports. The second type of user is someone who is already a frequent job-aid developer. The handbook presents new opportunities to use job aids to enhance performance—and new ways to develop and to deliver those aids.

If anyone had told me that I would be thinking, reading, and writing about something other than instruction, I would not have believed it. I now believe it. Information is a compelling tool. Job aids have much to contribute to effective people in effective organizations. This handbook is dedicated to helping readers to play significant roles in making that happen.

Allison Rossett
San Diego, California
April, 1991

Part One

Understanding Job Aids

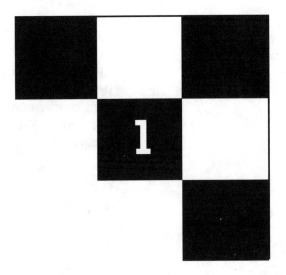

Introduction to Job Aids

They are everywhere. They adorn the top of the chalkboard in an elementary classroom, the underside of a stapler, the side of a mattress, and the inside of the cockpit of a DC-10.

They come in all shapes and sizes. One is a fading Post-it™ note marked "Water Me!!!" that is taped to an office fern; another is a laminated card in an emergency room that is meant to withstand errant sprays of blood and guts; another is a data-filled computer screen; and another is a smooth-voiced audiotape coach.

Some experts claim that these items can work wonders. They save money. They save time. They save marriages. They enhance training. They replace training. They improve performance. And they do all of these things at reduced costs to the organization.

What miracles are these that promise so much power at a fraction of the cost of other kinds of human-resource interventions? The answer is *job aids.* This chapter introduces and defines job aids and describes *A Handbook of Job Aids.*

What Is a Job Aid?

A job aid is a repository for information, processes, or perspectives that is external to the individual and that supports work and activity by directing, guiding, and enlightening performance. Each part of this definition can be examined more closely.

"Repository for information, processes, or perspectives." To be considered a job aid, the object in question—whether it be a poster, manual, tape, or computer program—must store and make accessible the information, processes, or perspectives on which effective human work and activity are based.

"External to the individual." Job aids get their identities, in part, by being separate from the individual. Job aids are found on shelves above employees' desks, on walls beside equipment and chemicals, in drawers beneath computer keyboards, within the bits and bytes of disk drives, underneath telephones, and on matchbook covers. Because job aids are separate and can be relied on when the need arises, the individual is not forced to rely on memory. For example, a manufacturing employee knows exactly what to do if he or she is exposed to hazardous chemicals because an oversize poster in proximity to both the chemicals and the shower lists the actions to take. A professor knows how to connect a long-distance conference call because a manual lists the steps required. A student knows how to get in touch with the man she met at a party because his telephone number is scribbled on a matchbook cover.

"Supports work and activity." Job aids play a role in all kinds of endeavors. To know how, when, and what, people often turn to documentation, guidelines, checklists, protocols, and references. Such tools help people to do their work, providing access to information, perspectives, procedures, policies, and examples. In settings as diverse as hospitals, mine fields, and hotels, job aids enable people to plan, to execute, and to evaluate work.

Job aids also support the more informal parts of people's lives. Cookbooks, shopping lists, to-do lists, personal calendars, planners, and address books all enable people to meet mundane and personal needs without committing information and details to memory.

"Directing, guiding, and enlightening performance." Sometimes a situation is so unforgiving that a specific response must be directed by a job aid. When display panels in

a nuclear-power plant indicate a problem, the operator's response must be precise, not flexible. The same is true for the preflight precautions taken by the crew of a commercial airliner. In many instances, a job aid tells an individual exactly what to do and in what order because the consequences of an error are too great to tolerate doing the task in any other way.

As guides, job aids provide steps, illustrations, and examples that keep performance on track. For example, creating a new voice message for a telephone answering machine is an occasional activity for many people; the steps are familiar but are not committed to memory. In this case, an illustrated document guides the user through the steps. As another example, a golfer who wants to coax extra yards from his or her swing can rely on a technological job aid in the form of a videotape player perched precariously on the golf cart. The golfer studies the model seconds before taking a swing, simultaneously watching the physical steps and listening to the verbal guidance of the expert.

Job aids enhance a person's perspective on and approach to a job. As resources for necessary information and guidance, they enhance enthusiasm and confidence. For example, the new burger chef at a fast-food restaurant feels better about those first few hours on the job because the procedures are posted in plain view.

In *The New Yorker*, a writer describes encountering an "instructive note about how not to have a breakdown" when the copy machine breaks down. Item 4 on the list taped to the machine reads "Please try not to take it personally when the machine has its problems... it's just a machine. In other words, please don't bang, beat, bruise, or otherwise abuse it. It won't help." No rules or instructions are given here; in this case the job aid provides gentle and comforting advice on how to handle the inevitable aggravations associated with using a copy machine.

What Is Not a Job Aid?

Not everything connected with a job is a job aid. For example, tools are not job aids and instruction is not a job aid.

Tools, like screwdrivers and office chairs, are often confused with job aids because they support people in their work. However, there is an important distinction between tools and job aids. The care tag on a mattress, a preflight checklist, and a computerized telephone directory are different from the office chair and the screwdriver because each is a repository for information. The support of work is necessary but not sufficient to make something a job aid. To qualify as a job aid, the device must serve as a place holder for information, processes, or perspectives.

Bookmarks, pencils, tractors, hard hats, and file cabinets are tools. User documentation, safety signs, and procedure lists are job aids. Although all of these items support the ability to perform effectively or safely, only the latter three store information and provide access to it.

A computer can be both a tool and a job aid. It is a tool when a salesperson uses it as a word processor and sends letters to prospective customers. The computer is a job aid when the salesperson uses its data base to provide information on prospects' purchasing histories in order to determine to whom a particular letter should be sent.

The distinction between instruction and job aids merits discussion. Instruction usually happens before a need arises and builds the capacity of the individual. Figure 1.1 illustrates the components of instruction. The individuals who participate in instruction, whether they be landscapers or surgeons, do so to develop their abilities to handle wide ranges of challenges.

Job aids, on the other hand, direct more immediate performance. They exert their influence as references *when the need to know arises*. A landscaper might turn to a reference manual to determine the watering needs of an unfamiliar plant, for example. Whereas instruction prepares people to act, job aids come into play when a person is faced with an

Instruction

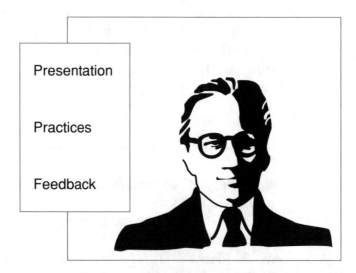

**Figure 1.1. Instruction Builds the
Capacity of the Individual**

immediate challenge. A job aid supports a person's performance when a computer disk is stuck in the drive, when instruments on a car's dashboard signal a significant problem, or when a customer asks to be referred to a Spanish-speaking salesperson with expertise in the culinary department.

Figure 1.2 illustrates the many job aids available to an office manager. This person not only carries a 3" x 5" card with notes for a presentation; the person also relies on numerous manuals, references, posters, computerized data bases, and checklists.

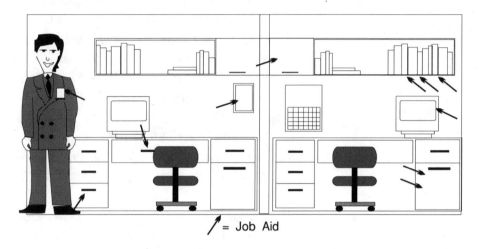

/ = Job Aid

Figure 1.2. Job Aids Available to an Office Manager

Instruction, in comparison, is a planned experience that enables an individual to acquire skills and knowledge that enhance his or her ability to perform. Instruction, an often laborious and costly process involving presentation, practice, and feedback, results in a change in the mental state of the individual. Later, organizations continue to draw on this expanded mental state by asking employees to manage, to create, to solve problems, and to anticipate.

The following scenario illustrates the naturally close connection between instruction and job aids:

Speedy Burger has invested in new equipment for cutting, stacking, and storing French fries in fast-food outlets across the country. At a regional meeting, store managers are introduced to a twenty-two-minute videotape and three laminated checklists designed to assist them in helping their employees to learn to use the new equipment. Each manager is asked to instruct his or her employees according to the following procedure:

1. *Set up the new machine with a good supply of potatoes.*
2. *Show the videotape.*
3. *Reiterate the safety issues highlighted in the videotape.*
4. *Elicit employee questions or concerns regarding safety or the procedure for making French fries.*
5. *Demonstrate loading by following the procedure outlined on the first laminated card.*
6. *Ask employees to work with partners and to load potatoes into the machine, following the procedure on the first laminated card.*
7. *Make certain that each of the partners has the opportunity to load the potatoes, using the procedure on the first laminated card.*
8. *Provide feedback to the employees and ask pairs who encountered problems to try the procedure again.*
9. *Demonstrate how to activate the machine, again reiterating safety concerns, and then ask an employee to try it.*
10. *Use the procedure outlined on the second laminated card to demonstrate how to take cut potatoes out of the machine, drawing attention once again to safety.*
11. *Ask half of the group to follow the procedure on the first card to load and activate the machine and the other half to remove cut potatoes by following the procedure on the second card.*
12. *Provide feedback and then ask the individuals to exchange cards and roles.*
13. *Elicit questions.*
14. *Remind employees about the popularity of French fries and their importance to the business, the benefits to be derived from use of the new machine, and the importance of safety features. Show them where the laminated cards will be posted.*
15. *After employees have returned to their work, introduce the third laminated card to assistant store managers. This card lists daily and weekly*

maintenance tasks and illustrates necessary steps. Demonstrate maintenance tasks by following the procedures listed on the card and then ask each assistant manager to do the same. Provide feedback on each person's performance and reiterate the importance of maintenance to safety, productivity, and cleanliness. Remind the assistant store managers of the importance of coaching employees.

This is a familiar example of blending training and job aids to prepare individuals to rely on job aids. In this scenario, employees and managers receive oral and video orientations to the new equipment, with an emphasis on purposes, benefits, and safety. As part of training, employees are taught to use the procedures outlined on the job aids (the laminated cards) to load and unload potatoes. In addition, a third job aid is introduced to support assistant store managers in maintenance tasks.

Figure 1.3 provides another illustration of this familiar combination. In the figure, employees are being trained to

Figure 1.3. How Job Aids Influence the Introduction of New Work Technologies and Systems

operate a new software system. The training session includes presentations, opportunities for practice and feedback, and guided demonstrations on the uses of the on-line help system. The computerized help system is itself an electronic job aid. When the need arises, the help system provides the user with specific information in response to queries. The user does not need to memorize procedures or refer to print documentation; the necessary information resides within the new software. When the employees return to the work site, they will be familiar with work that relies on these job aids because the aids were an integral part of training. This scenario illustrates the ways that job aids, in conjunction with training and supervisory support, play key roles in the introduction of new work technologies and systems.

A Handbook of Job Aids

Goals

This handbook has two major goals:

1. To serve as a "job aid on job aids"; and
2. To define job aids in new and expanded ways that broaden the opportunities for their use and that improve the quality of the job aids that are developed.

The handbook is meant to make the reader's life easier and to stimulate thought, reading, and new directions for action. This will be a book about job aids and a book that becomes a job aid itself. Later, when the need arises, developers will come back to this book to seek out descriptions, ideas, examples, and caveats.

Intended Audience

This handbook was written for people who are responsible for improving the way that people do their work. Many are called trainers; others are known as technical writers, instructional designers, human resources managers, personnel managers, course developers, education specialists, and documentation coordinators. What they have in common is that they are charged with helping people in their organizations to become competent in responding to requests, changes, innovations, products, customers, and problems.

Initially, the handbook was written only for these full-time human performance professionals. However, friends and colleagues from other arenas (city government, psychological services, and small businesses) looked at the chapters and pointed out applications to their own situations. For example, a psychologist saw ways to use job aids in simplifying and standardizing the training she does for psychology assistants. An attorney thought of ways to use job aids in preparing witnesses to testify in court. The coordinator of several dozen part-time sales people described ways to use job aids in keeping her workers up-to-date on new products and services—without taking them away from selling for training.

Thus the vision of the audience for the handbook was broadened to include both full-time professionals and those who count education, training, and information as only portions of their jobs. The writing, organization, and examples are suited to the serious student of the topic, the experienced developer of job aids, and the person who is creating a job aid for the first time.

Format

A Handbook of Job Aids has four parts. Part One introduces and defines job aids. It provides background for this work, articulates traditional definitions and opportunities for using job aids, and explains how the handbook breaks new ground.

Part Two is the heart of the book. It presents specific formats for job aids and detailed steps for developing them.

Part Three comprises examples and commentaries. Although examples and discussions occur throughout the handbook, Part Three is devoted exclusively to them. It is organized according to the three types of job aids (informing, proceeding, and coaching) and presents actual examples of job aids, enriched by comments and suggestions from the developers themselves.

Part Four focuses on the emerging trends in organizations and on the implications of these trends and new technologies for performance support. The handbook concludes with a summary and an agenda for research and development.

Each chapter begins with problems, quotes, or anecdotes that highlight and prepare the reader for the ideas and examples to come. Each chapter closes with a comprehensive review of content, a brief preview of the next chapter, and appropriate resources and references.

Review of Chapter 1

Definition of job aids.

■ Repositories for information, processes, or perspectives that are external to the individual and that support work and activity by directing, guiding, and enlightening performance.

Key features of job aids.

- Job aids exist in the environment, apart from the individual.
- Job aids are called on by the performer when a challenge arises.
- Job aids serve as storehouses for information and perspectives.
- Job aids signal when and how to perform.
- Job aids diminish a person's reliance on memory.
- Job aids exist in diverse formats, such as notes, posters, and protocols.
- Job aids have the potential to contribute to work and nonwork aspects of life.

Comparisons.

- Although both job aids and tools support performance, only job aids store information for easy access by the individual. User documentation, checklists, and safety posters are examples of job aids. A stapler and a portable vacuum are examples of tools.
- Instruction is the preparation to perform, usually happening before the individual is challenged. Job aids are more immediate and specific references; people turn to them as they need them.
- Management development is an example of instruction because it is devoted to building the internal capacity of the individual. A job aid that supports a manager might be a checklist of characteristics to keep in mind when preparing a performance review for a subordinate.

A Handbook of Job Aids.

- The goals are to be useful to practitioners and to offer an intriguing and meaningful conceptualization for job aids.
- The intended audience is professionals in personnel and human resources as well as others in the organization who are charged with improving performance.

Preview of Chapter 2

Chapter 2 answers the following questions: "What is so great about job aids? Why all the fuss? Why a handbook devoted to them? Why are they everywhere? And where did they come from?"

References

Duncan, C.S. (1985). Job aids really can work: A study of the military applications of job aid technology. *Performance and Instruction, 24*(4), 1-4.

Duncan, C.S. (1986). Commentary: The job aid has a future. In *Introduction to Performance Technology* (pp. 125-128). Washington, DC: National Society for Performance and Instruction.

Finnegan, G.T. (1985). Job aids: Improving employee performance in healthcare. *Performance and Instruction, 24*(6), 10-11.

Harless, J.H. (1986). Guiding performance with job aids. In *Introduction to Performance Technology* (pp. 106-124). Washington, DC: National Society for Performance and Instruction.

Lineberry, C.S., & Bullock, D.H. (1980). Job aids. In L. Lipsitz (Ed.), *The Instructional Design Library.* Englewood Cliffs, NJ: Educational Technology Publications.

Mockovak, W.P. (1983). Integrating training and manual design using job aids. *Educational Technology, 23*(2), 21-23.

Nelson, J. (1989). Quick and dirty job aids. *Performance and Instruction, 28*(6), 35-36.

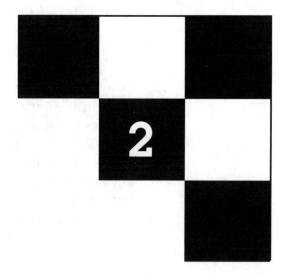

The Benefits of Job Aids

"Sure, you say they're the best thing since sliced bread. But, really, what is so great about job aids? What do they do for us? Why are they everywhere?"

"Is there a down side that we should consider? Does the use of job aids raise other issues?"

"Are job aids new? Where do job aids come from?"

Chapter 2 addresses these questions by covering the following two topics:

- The benefits of job aids; and
- The drawbacks of job aids.

Job aids are not new. People have relied on job aids since prehistoric times, when the details of fire tending, skinning, and cooking adorned cave walls. In more contemporary times, a study of military reliance on job aids between 1958 and 1972 (Duncan, 1985) documents their ongoing, significant, and positive contributions to military training. The military's use of systematic approaches to the design of training (using the Interservice Procedures for Instructional Systems Development) influenced civilian business practices, as did their reliance on job aids. Bolstered by constant change, new technologies, and less-skilled entry-level workers, job aids today are making increasingly significant contributions to performance improvement in government, business, social services, and even public education. This trend will continue.

A review of the literature and feedback from practitioners present a rosy picture of the benefits of job aids. In this chapter, the benefits of job aids are explored from four different perspectives: the organizational bottom line, the individual, the nature of work, and the training process.

Impact on the Bottom Line

Harless (1986), often acknowledged as the father of job aids, says that job aids save the organization money. In speeches, presentations, and articles, with a certainty that comes from scores of successful consulting projects involving the use of job aids; Harless states that job aids can be developed in three to five times less time than it takes to develop equivalent training programs. He also points out instances in which the use of job aids diminished the need for training, thereby shortening the amount of time that employees were away from their jobs.

Harless is not alone in his certainty that job aids have a positive effect on the bottom line. Duncan (1985) concurs, citing a review of military research studies on the impact of job aids; the results of these analyses showed overwhelmingly that job aids saved money without jeopardizing work performance.

The notion that job aids save money makes sense. Consider the example of the new potato-cutting machine in Chapter 1, a new software program, or a new set of personnel policies. How much time would it take to provide sufficient presentations, practices, and feedback to enable employees to memorize the necessary information, concepts, and procedures? It would take a great deal of time and a significant investment of resources. Job aids enable employees to go elsewhere for this information, swiftly and appropriately—to laminated cards, user documentation, or policy manuals. Because job aids are a storehouse for essential information that need not be deposited in the human mind through the costly process of training, they have the potential to save the organization money.

Impact on the Individual

Job aids, as personal support systems that are close at hand, help people to do their work better and to feel better about their work. For example, job aids can serve as memory joggers. For instance, an administrative assistant might once have known how to use a word-processing program to format and to create columns; that subject had been covered in a training class, but the job has not required the use of columns for two months. Instead of feeling self-conscious about having forgotten or bothering someone else in the office, the administrative assistant can open up the software documentation and follow the procedure outlined there. This administrative assistant has permission to forget. In fact, the software developers anticipated that people would forget and created the job aid in response to the anticipated need. The job aid boosts the likelihood that the administrative assistant will successfully accomplish the task—and feel competent in the process.

Sometimes individuals cannot be expected to know how to do a task. This is the case when the activity is very complex (such as determining the factory's need for raw materials), very critical (such as troubleshooting life-support equipment), or infrequently performed (such as cleaning the heads on a videocassette recorder). Individuals also cannot be expected to know how to do something if they lack the prerequisite skills and educational backgrounds. Consider the hotel employee for whom English is a second language. That worker can receive a significant boost from job aids that make certain that he or she completes all the steps needed to check a guest into the hotel.

Sometimes job aids provide support to employees who have been placed in jobs that are a "big stretch" for them. A good example of this is the print and computerized support that is often provided to loan officers. Job aids prompt them through difficult processes and decisions, substituting for experience or training.

Individuals also cannot be expected to rely on their own memories when the information, procedures, or policies change frequently, as in the case of product prices or high-technology product features. In such situations, job aids help employees to adjust to the reduced shelf life of information and the continual insertion of new technologies.

Job aids also help employees to manage vast quantities of information. A simple example is the number of telephone directories that have been forced into two and even three separate books. A more complex example is the trend toward computerized data bases; at many university libraries, the familiar card-catalog trays are being replaced by automated-search systems.

Finally, a change in a job or its technology may be so simple that it does not warrant explanations, demonstrations, practices, and feedback. Such changes can be communicated via job aids, as in the case of the automated potato-cutting machine.

In the midst of rapid change, employee turnover, absence of skills, large data bases, critical outcomes, and absentmindedness, job aids offer support. They lend information, direction, and guidance, so that individuals are able to remain cool, confident, and competent. The challenges for the workers of the 1990s are formidable. One consolation is that they confront these challenges armed with job aids.

Impact on the Nature of Work

Experts agree that the United States has moved from the Industrial Age to the Information Age. Les Thurow, Dean of the Massachusetts Institute of Technology's Sloan School of Management, makes the case that standards of living rise not because people work harder but because they work smarter and that economic progress represents the replacement of physical exertion with brain power.

Job aids, delivered through print and emergent technologies, expand the meaning of the phrase *brain power.* No longer are workers competent because they "know it cold." Now workers often express their competence by knowing the difference between what they know and do not know and then by knowing how to access appropriate data, information, knowledge, and perspectives.

Jobs that are knowledge intensive are everywhere, not just in the service sector. Clancy (1989) writes the following:

> American manufacturing has started a slow process of evolution toward the factory of the future. Many manufacturing companies are replacing single purpose workers and machines with multiskilled workers and multipurpose machines.... In that process, the number of levels and job classifications within the company often decreases. On the other hand, responsibilities at the remaining levels, especially the lower levels, increase significantly.... Workers in each cell must have the skills to operate a variety of machines, the ability to control the manufacturing environments of diverse products, and the knowledge to manage people, the process and the various product requirements. (p. 46)

Manufacturing employees, then, are asked to shift from responsibility for the manual assembly of a piece to the broader responsibilities of a worker whose lathe is replaced or supported by an automated work station. Other kinds of employees also will be expected to rely on work stations. For example, work stations will enable telephone-repair personnel to sense and to diagnose phone problems from a distance; other work stations will enable social workers to locate parents who fail to pay child support. Work stations gain significant portions of their usefulness by housing job aids with print and electronic links to data bases and expertise.

As reliance on work stations grows and as the technology to support this reliance develops, more workers will earn their livings at home and in other remote locations. Job aids will play a role in assuring equal availability of information and consistency of performance across sites and distances.

Exemplary job performance in scores of job classifications has grown to include inquiry skills, critical thinking, decision making, anticipation, and a focus on quality. The successful organization will be the one that acknowledges these growing responsibilities and provides dependable support, often in the form of job aids, for the individual to adapt to radical changes in the nature of work.

Impact on Training

Job aids contribute to the human resource development (HRD) function in the following ways:

Clarity. Training and development professionals, line managers, and subject-matter experts should answer key questions before employing job aids: What do employees need to know? In detail, what are the skills, knowledge, and perspectives that are essential? What goals and objectives must be achieved? What information or action makes a difference? What are the policies, procedures, or approaches that are essential? Effective job aids cannot be written for undefined content, intangible goals, or murky purposes. Job aids provide the best service when concerned parties have agreed on solid definitions and clear intentions. Recently, a colleague in the nuclear industry illustrated the point in this conversation: "I can't talk now. I'm frantic. Four working days from now, I'm supposed to be running a training session on a job aid that hasn't been developed yet. Why hasn't it been developed? Well, the organization can't decide what it needs to say to supervisors regarding compliance and observation for a certain kind of environmental safety monitoring.

No policies, no procedures, and no approaches, so no job aid and no training. What am I going to tell those supervisors?"

Less Training. Job aids promise to reduce the length of training. They do reduce the length of training—in a way. If the content and objectives are held stable—that is, if no more skills, knowledge, or perspectives are added—then training time can be reduced through job aids. However, as the nature of work expands, training is pressed to have more impact on the individual in the same period of time. This is where job aids can help. Research findings support the contention that training can be reduced when job aids supplant or supplement instructor-led training.

Quality of Training. Time within a training session that is devoted to introducing and coaching people on the use of job aids is likely to be perceived as relevant to actual work, both by the employees and by their supervisors. During a classroom practice exercise, if salespeople are asked to use reference manuals to check product and peripheral compatibilities, they are likely to perceive the training to be very much like the kind of challenges they confront when selling. Similarly, if case workers are being trained in eligibility requirements, their training should include constant references to the hardware and software that help them make decisions at their work stations.

Transfer of Training. Job aids help employees to transfer their skills from the classroom to the work site. The Speedy Burger example in Chapter 1 illustrates this point: Employee familiarity with and reliance on job aids is included as part of the manager's presentation. Then the same job aids accompany the employee back to the kitchen and the demands of french-fry cutting and cooking. Increasing the common elements between the classroom and the job increases the likelihood of skill transfer and improves work performance.

Transfer of Personnel. Based on his research, Duncan (1985) reports that maintenance personnel who have been trained with job aids transfer more effectively from one type of operation to another.

Revision of Training. Although it is not easy to retrieve and revise existing job aids, this approach is much easier than altering the skills and knowledge that reside in the mind of each employee. In addition, revisions are made easier by the increasing reliance on computers in organizations. With a few keystrokes, people can bring job aids up-to-date and then disseminate the information electronically.

Expanded Roles for Training and Development Practitioners. Many people believe that the job of an HRD practitioner is to provide whatever an organization requests. Too often this belief has resulted in an attempt to use training for challenges that training cannot solve. The planning, development, and use of job aids has the potential to contribute to an expanded perception of the following aspects of HRD:

1. That HRD is based on needs assessment, a systematic inquiry process that analyzes learners, jobs, and subject matter prior to recommending or implementing appropriate solutions.

2. That different kinds of problems and challenges should be addressed by different solutions. Figure 2.1 makes this point by pairing problems and interventions.

3. That solutions are usually multifaceted; involve whole systems; and include potential changes in job descriptions, tools, job aids, training, and incentives.

KINDS OF PROBLEMS	KINDS OF INTERVENTIONS
Lack of skills/knowledge	Training Job aids Coaching and mentoring
Flawed incentives	New policies New contracts Training for supervisors
Flawed environment	Work redesign New and better tools Better matches between jobs and people
Lack of motivation	Information about benefits Testimonials regarding value Training to build confidence

Figure 2.1. Matching Problems with Interventions

Thus far, job aids appear to be just about the perfect solution to every performance challenge. That is not true. In fact, their use raises other issues, many of which relate more to the realities of people's roles within organizations than to flaws inherent in job aids.

Job Aids and the Reward Structure

In many organizations, the training budget is tied to the following two figures: the number of individuals who attend training and the length of time they are there. Boosting these figures boosts resources and lowering them diminishes funding. As a result, HRD professionals are penalized for needs assessments that result in fewer bodies in classrooms and greater reliance on job aids.

In addition, more training units are being pressed to become profit centers within their organizations. Therefore, they confront the problem of how to charge for job aids. Although there are time-honored ways of accounting for the costs of sending employees to classes, there are no such means for figuring out what a job aid is worth. One telecommunications professional described a situation in which he had labored for nearly two weeks to develop a four-page job aid that was duplicated and disseminated to hundreds of employees. He was both gratified at the popularity of his work and saddened that his department was unable to recapture the cost of his efforts.

Job Aids and Organizational Structure

The people who are charged with training and development are often housed in a unit that is separate and distinct from the people responsible for developing documentation, data bases, and methodology statements. This makes the development and use of job aids more difficult than it might otherwise be. It is not impossible, but it is difficult.

A recent training seminar for a public utility illustrated this point. The majority of the people in the audience were course developers, eager to study needs-assessment techniques so that they could create better courses. Also in the class were three individuals representing the documentation group. The course developers and documentation writers did not know each other. Their worlds were separate. Not only did they come to the course from separate units; they also traveled from different regions of the country. The results of the course and their interactions were that course developers became excited about job aids and their potential within and as an adjunct to instructor-led classes. Simultaneously, the documentation writers became more conscious of the training necessary to support the introduction of job aids. All agreed that it was essential to launch projects with needs assessment and that they needed to collaborate to improve employee performance.

A positive trend is reflected by the organizational pattern in Education Services at Digital Equipment Corporation. One person manages a large group that includes course development and documentation. If the overarching goal is to improve performance, then education and information must work together—strategically, programmatically, and organizationally.

Job Aids and Floods of Paper

Although job aids are wonderful, their production and dissemination increase the amount of paper that surrounds employees. A colleague told about visiting a nuclear-power plant. He was impressed by the quality of the very modern and technological control room. Everything appeared to be perfect until he glanced at the feet of the employees. They were up to their ankles in manuals and updates. Although no money or design expertise had been spared in the development of the room, the planners apparently forgot how heavily job-aided and documented the work would be and its resulting effects on the environment.

There is no easy solution to this problem. Careful needs assessment should lead to development of job aids when appropriate and no more often than that. It is also useful to anticipate when floods of paper will be necessary and to develop supportive office, work space, notebook, filing, and revision systems. In addition, as workers move toward a more paperless workplace, with heavier reliance on computers and computerized work stations, the flood of papers will be replaced by on-line files, hard-disk storage, file servers, and CD-ROM devices.

Job Aids and Inappropriate Simplification

Job aids force people to be clear. However, job aids also can encourage people to make inappropriate simplifications. The following is a conversation that took place at a company in Texas:

Training Director (TD): What we're looking for is a course for our course developers on needs assessment—something that will help them do a better job of responding to requests for assistance from other departments.

Training Manager (TM): I was hoping for something that could be delivered in two or three days. We want a focus on building skills.

Allison Rossett (AR): Why do you think you need this course?

TM: Our developers aren't doing a good job of responding to line managers.

AR: How do you know they're not doing a good job?

TM: They need to be told how to respond. When you go out and talk to them, there are forty different opinions on how to conduct a needs assessment.

TD: I'd like to see us try to do this with a job aid, supported by some training, of course. If you really nail this topic down, you ought to teach the needs-assessment steps, say six or eight of them, put them in the job aid, demonstrate the job aid for them and then set them loose. We'd save some significant training time right there.

This is a classic example of inappropriate simplification. Although there are certainly some signposts—perhaps more aptly called billboards—representative of broad steps in the needs-assessment process, the ability to do an effective needs assessment cannot be reduced to procedures. As useful as job aids are, they can and should play only bit parts in supporting the work of the brain surgeon, golf-course designer, psychologist, or judge.

It is essential that trainers carefully select opportunities for the use of job aids. Although this handbook expands and illustrates those opportunities, it also cautions against leaping to the conclusion that job aids can replace education and training for the development of insight and judgment.

Job Aids Cost   The success of job aids depends on how they look and read and whether they capture "the right stuff." Is the job aid user friendly? Is it easier to look for information in the documentation or decision table than it is to call a colleague? Does it answer the user's questions?

Developing a job aid that results in affirmative answers to these questions costs money. Although experts agree that using job aids costs less than developing training to achieve equivalent objectives, job aids still cost something. The resources that must be allocated to needs assessment remain. To that cost is added the cost of selecting formats, designing, purchasing graphics expertise, producing the aids in a durable format, programming (when appropriate), disseminating, revising, controlling, and managing the process.

Too often these costs are forgotten. For example, a vendor contracted to deliver computer-based training, print documentation, and job aids for the purpose of training salespeople about computer-supported sales. The vendor developed excellent computer-based training. However, despite the fact that the client had specified job aids in the form of print documentation and small desktop flip charts, the vendor had taken those into account only casually. As soon as the computerized training was completed, the project manager and key staff turned their attention to something more "sexy." Other staff members hurriedly completed the job aids, and the quality of the entire project dimmed.

Another significant cost factor is what it will take to support the initial use of the aids. Remember that some form of informing or training usually accompanies their introduction. The minimum support is a memo or letter that explains the importance and role of the job aid. In other cases, support may come in the form of a training session. More extensive support, involving hours and even days, may be essential for success in the case of learning to use new work stations. If employees are accustomed to relying on job aids, they will need less training on when and how to use them. The skills and habits associated with the use of one job aid will generalize to others, especially if similar formats are involved.

Review of Chapter 2

Chapter 2 reviewed the benefits of job aids and the drawbacks of them.

The benefits of job aids.

- Job aids save money and time;
- Job aids help people to do their jobs better;
- Job aids help people feel better about new and challenging jobs;
- Job aids ensure more consistent performance across divisions and distances;

- Job aids address the challenges of less-skilled employees and rapid turnover;
- Job aids force their creators to be clear about the nature of the job and the skills and knowledge associated with it;
- Job aids diminish reliance on memory;
- Job aids support decision making, critical thinking, and access to varied sources of knowledge and opinions;
- Job aids compel their designers to be clear about how organizations want jobs to be done;
- Job aids increase the relevance of training;
- Job aids support cross-training, the ability of people to transfer positions and responsibilities more readily; and
- Job aids expand the perception and role of human resource development professionals.

The drawbacks of job aids.

- Job aids raise questions about resources;
- Job aids raise questions about costs for their development and dissemination;
- Job aids increase floods of paper in an organization;
- Job aids can foster oversimplification; and
- Job aids are not free, although professionals often forget to budget sufficient amounts to support their development and implementation.

Preview of Chapter 3

Chapter 3 describes when job aids are appropriate to use and when they are inappropriate.

References

Clancy, J.A. (1989). Training workers for the factory of the future. *Training and Development Journal, 43*(2), 46-49.

Duncan, C.S. (1985). Job aids really can work: A study of the military applications of job aid technology. *Performance and Instruction, 24*(4), 1-4.

Duncan, C.S. (1986). Commentary: The job aid has a future. In *Introduction to Performance Technology* (pp. 125-128). Washington, DC: National Society for Performance and Instruction.

Harless, J.H. (1986). Guiding performance with job aids. In *Introduction to Performance Technology* (pp. 106-124). Washington, DC: National Society for Performance and Instruction.

Pipe, P. (1986). Ergonomics and performance aids. In *Introduction to Performance Technology* (pp. 129-144). Washington, DC: National Society for Performance and Instruction.

Rossett, A. (1987). *Training needs assessment.* Englewood Cliffs, NJ: Educational Technology Publications.

Rossett, A. (1989). Assess for success. *Training and Development Journal, 43*(5), 55-59.

Rossett, A. (1990). Overcoming obstacles to needs assessment. *Training: The Magazine of Human Resources Development, 27* (3), 36-41.

Tovar, R., Rossett, A., & Carter, N. (1989). Centralized training services in a decentralized organization. *Training and Development Journal, 43*(2), 62-65.

When to Use Job Aids

How can Brett, sales-training manager for a company that sells computer peripherals, use job aids to help his people sell nearly ninety different products, each of which has numerous and changing features and compatibilities?

What opportunities does Jeannette, training director at a large hotel with turnover problems, have to use job aids to improve performance?

How might Miguel use job aids to support management and leadership effectiveness within his organization, particularly as it takes on a new approach to employee involvement?

Chapter 3 provides guidance for these situations by answering the following two questions:

- When is it appropriate to use job aids?
- And when is it not appropriate to use job aids?

When Is It Appropriate to Use Job Aids?

If people could remember everything, then job aids would not be necessary. Job aids are used largely because of limitations on memory.

Memory can be categorized in two ways: long-term memory (LTM) and short-term memory (STM). Long-term memory represents information that is stored, encoded, and retained in the brain as associations and networks. Memories are stored in LTM, whether they are recollections about chopping down Christmas trees with Grandpa, the political history of Malta versus Yalta, the definition of "pusillanimous," or a favorite brand of virgin olive oil.

The movement of information from STM into LTM, into meaningful networks, is called *learning*. It costs time and money to support people as they learn; learning requires that their exposures to people, things, and data change from random and fleeting memories to memories that are organized, meaningful, and retained. The time and effort required to learn multiplication tables is a good example of that movement of information from STM into LTM.

Short-term memory (also referred to as working memory) is limited, usually to five to seven pieces of information. A good illustration of the limits on STM is the process of transferring a credit-card number from a bill to the check that will pay the bill. Some people capture four numbers at a time; others can capture five, six, seven, or as many as eight numbers. People differ in the number of times they have to go back to the credit card before they can reproduce the account number. And people get annoyed when they have to record or transfer even longer numbers. The problem comes from the limits of memory and the memory decay that occurs when people rely on STM.

Because STM has limited capacity and because moving data into LTM requires resources, professionals concerned with effective performance are confronted with a challenge. Should they spend the time and resources needed to do what it will take to enable people to know their jobs by heart? Given the quantities and the changing nature of information associated with work, is it possible to memorize significant portions of a job? More and more, the answer to both questions is "no." Instead, people rely on job aids.

In support of this position, Clark (1986) makes the following recommendation:

> Designers should encourage learners to use working memory to *process* information, *not* to store it. For example, as learners first practice a new procedure, give them access to clear written summary steps for reference so all working memory can be directed toward executing the procedure. The use of job aids, in the form of a written procedure table in this instance, can be especially power-

ful for this purpose. With enough repetition of the task, it will become automatic and bypass working memory. Then the job aid will become unnecessary. (p. 19)

People choose job aids in the following situations:

1. When the performance is infrequent. Job aids should be used when an individual cannot be expected to remember how to do something he or she rarely does. Whether people rely on aids to provide the details of an acquaintance's address or to compare product specifications or to carry out the procedure for cleaning the heads on a videocassette recorder, job aids boost infrequent performance.

2. When the situation is complex, has multiple steps, or has multiple attributes. There is no question about the increasing complexity and government regulation surrounding the world of work. Job aids now support individuals who confront lengthy, difficult, and information-intensive challenges. How does an employee secure data in a computer system so that certain employees have access to those data but others do not? How do employees activate new features of the numerical-control lathe? What factors must a manager keep in mind when terminating an employee? Many employers choose to answer these questions by providing job aids.

3. When the consequences of errors are high. The following are examples of such situations:

- A salesperson promises compatibility between an existing mainframe computer system and a large new system; a client purchases the new system and finds it incompatible.
- An accountant initializes a computer disk and in the process deletes a client's financial history.
- A commercial jet-maintenance employee fails to notice that a fuel tank is nearly empty, although its gauge shows nearly a full tank.
- An employee uses a computerized analysis to classify and to match blood types and is not sure exactly how to do it.

In each of these circumstances, reliance on job aids is indicated because the situations do not allow for errors.

4. When performance depends on a large body of information. Getting work done in the "Information Age" depends on ready access to large amounts of information on people, places, things, and policies. With access to references ranging from the Yellow Pages to the extraordinary capacities of

CD-ROM and CD-Interactive, individuals will increasingly rely on print and automated job aids to answer questions about who, what, when, and where.

5. *When performance is dependent on knowledge, procedures, or approaches that change frequently.* Information challenges transcend large data sets; they extend also to the shelf life of knowledge, procedures, and approaches. In the past, an employee could feel relatively comfortable after settling into a position. That is no longer true. For instance, the contemporary salesperson must stay abreast of changing products, features, and compatibilities.

6. *When employee performance can be improved through self-assessment and correction with new or emphasized standards in mind.* This book proposes expanded roles for job aids. For example, a highway-maintenance employee can become more safety conscious under snow conditions immediately after reading a document that provides coaching on the unique aspects of that situation. Similarly, a manager can conduct a more sensitive performance appraisal after referring to an automated job aid with reminders about what to keep in mind during the interview. A trainer is likely to return to the classroom with heightened skills if, during the lunch break, he or she has pondered the morning's teaching efforts in light of a structured checklist on desirable instructional strategies.

7. *When there is high turnover and the task is simple.* Organizations are less willing to invest in training when employees are considered to be temporary and the performance challenge is judged to be minimal. For example, a woman publishes a small, commercial directory of goods and services. Her sales force is active for only a few months each year, turns over frequently, and handles a very simple product line with a rate card that does not change frequently. She relies on job aids because she wants her salespeople in the field, not at training sessions.

8. *When there is little time or few resources to devote to training.* This is a "real-world" book; as such, it acknowledges that organizations often turn to job aids when they are unable to expend resources on education and training. Job aids become popular when resources are scarce. However, in certain circumstances, job aids will do more harm than good; these situations are described in the next section.

If any one of these eight circumstances exists, the training or HRD professional should *consider* job aids. Note the use of the word "consider." The use of job aids is not an open-and-shut case. Sometimes—even when the material is complex, the outcome is critical, and training resources are limited—a practitioner still will not want to use job aids or may need to rely on a combination of training and job aids.

When Is It Not Appropriate to Use Job Aids?

Job aids are not appropriate in certain situations; the sections that follow outline some guidelines for circumstances in which a training and development professional might choose not to use job aids.

When job aids damage credibility. Suppose a person has the following symptoms: slight fever, headache, stuffy nose, and sore throat. During a visit to a family physician, the doctor listens to those symptoms; thinks about them for a few seconds; and reaches for a large, heavy medical textbook. Now suppose the person has different symptoms: slight fever; headache; stuffy nose; sore throat; spots in front of the eyes; and a rash on the chest, palms, and the soles of the feet. During a visit to another family physician, that doctor listens to those symptoms; thinks about them for a few seconds; and reaches for a large, heavy medical text.

Which doctor would the person prefer? Which inspires confidence? Most people would choose the second physician, who refers to references for more unusual challenges rather than for the basics of daily medical practice.

Individuals are expected to be knowledgeable about topics and questions they confront with regularity. Only when the inquiry is unusual, irregular, complex, or infrequent might a professional refer to other sources without others' questioning the professional's competence. People expect others to be "smart," to have their jobs down cold, and to really know what they are doing, especially if those others are professionals like engineers, doctors, management consultants, financial advisors, pilots, and school principals. These people and many others are expected to respond to typical challenges without referring to other sources.

Human resource development professionals need to ask, "If people see this individual in the act of referring to other sources, will they question the person's skills or knowledge?" If the answer is yes, then education and training, not job aids, must be used to enhance performance.

When speedy performance is a priority. What kinds of circumstances necessitate speedy performance? The following two situations are most common: (1) when the organization places a very high value on throughput, the processing of a large number of products or people; or (2) when life or limb hangs in the balance. Although retail and financial organizations rely on job aids for many situations, they prefer their people to know many of the recurring aspects of their jobs by heart. Why? They want tellers, branch managers, salespeople, and customer-service representatives to be able to do large quantities of business in short periods of time. If requests for assistance or information necessitate reference to manual job aids, the number of contacts declines, affecting the bottom line.

Speed is crucial during medical or equipment emergencies. Some emergency responses are supported by job aids; others are not. The decision to rely on job aids depends on how quickly the performance must occur. If instantaneous response is essential and there is not time to seek instructions from a manual, poster, or computer program, such as in the case of immediate evacuations or responses to airplane emergencies, then employees must be trained to perform automatically and by heart. Because dire emergencies are rare in most lines of work, training must be repeated on a regular basis.

When novel and unpredictable situations are involved. Job aids are not particularly good as supports for individuals who confront novel and largely unpredictable circumstances. Such situations demand intangible abilities to handle surprises, stresses, and new challenges. School districts expect good judgment from employees when they are confronted by parents who are hysterical about their children's test results; the Navy also expects good judgment from pilots when they are subjected to combat situations. Brecke (1982) explored the topic of training to instill judgment in pilots. He provided a useful definition of judgment as the "right stuff" evoked in situations that include uncertainty, lack of complete information, stress, task difficulty, cognitive complexity, and time constraints. Brecke complained that military training in 1982 was characterized by an emphasis on correct completion of prescribed procedures and compliance with rules. Although compliance with procedures can be comfortably supported by job aids, it is not likely to clinch victory in the skies. That victory is the result of good judgment. If good judgment in a topsy-turvy world is a goal, job aids will not be major players in ensuring the high end of that kind of performance.

When smooth and fluid performance is a top priority. World-class athletes, for example, do not refer to job aids. Imagine Martina Navratilova in a confrontation with a tough opponent in the finals of a major tennis tournament. The crowd is hushed, the wind comes up, and rain begins to fall. During the change of sides, Navratilova reaches into her bag to consult a laminated card with suggestions on how to prevail in high wind and light rain. Using job aids would appear ridiculous in this situation, just as it would in the case of a prima ballerina, a veteran surgeon, or a master teacher. Interrupting the flow of such an effort to refer to reference materials is preposterous. Successful performance in these cases is dependent on habitual, automatic, flexible, and seamless performance. The design of the job in these situations is incongruous with the use of a job aid.

When the employee lacks sufficient reading, listening, or reference skills. The HRD professional who is considering designing a job aid needs to answer the following questions:

- Which individuals are going to be using the job aid?
- Are these people accustomed to turning to sources outside themselves for information?
- Can they read? If so, at what level?
- Do they know how to read flow charts, diagrams, charts, and illustrations?
- Are they comfortable with computers and their uses as sources of information?
- How good are their listening skills? Will they take the time to listen to the guidelines provided by an audio job aid?

Revisiting Brett, Jeannette, and Miguel

This chapter began with questions about how three professionals might use job aids. Here are some suggestions for them:

Brett, the computer sales manager, must make extensive product references available to his salespeople because their success depends on their knowledge of products that are complex and changing. There is no way that he can expect salespeople to memorize this essential and volatile information. In addition, Brett does not want his company to be liable for inaccuracies. Therefore, he must provide job aids that offer ready access to features, compatibilities, comparisons, and prices. Although print references are standard support systems for salespeople, Brett should consider an on-line product-knowledge system. Geographical distances, accuracy, and immediate updates would be facilitated by electronic provision of information. An added bonus would be that the credibility of people who sell computer peripherals would be enhanced by their command of and reliance on technology as a sales tool.

Jeannette, training director at the hotel, relies on job aids as a primary method for enhancing employee performance. Employees responsible for uncomplicated tasks change jobs often. Thus she should develop checklists for new employees on everything from laundry procedures to concierge services. Job aids provide on-the-job support for new employees; the process of developing job aids also helps management to clarify the policies and procedures associated with laundry, concierge, and all the other services of the hotel. Veteran employees also should receive job-aid support, particularly when confronting unusual requests or complicated, infrequently performed procedures. For example, the person at the hotel's front desk might use a job aid regarding valet and special-service requests. New, computerized, point-of-sales registers are available for food and beverage services that include built-in information about prices and a warning system to alert supervisors when supplies are running low or the system is malfunctioning.

Miguel, training manager at a social-service agency, cannot stretch his budget to provide leadership training for supervisors and managers. Because his organization is changing to emphasize quality and employee participation, Miguel might turn to job aids to coach supervisors and managers in new ways of handling the challenge of performance reviews. Miguel and key upper-level managers might select performance appraisals as an arena in which to use job aids. They then would develop coaching guides and checklists for managers to read as they planned appraisals, filled out forms, conducted appraisal interviews, and handled related grievances. The job aids would reflect the new participative organizational philosophy and would be an initial step in an effort to innovate.

Review of Chapter 3

Use job aids in the following situations:

- When the performance is infrequent;
- When the situation is complex;
- When the consequences of error are very high;
- When success depends on access to vast and/or changing bodies of knowledge;
- When the job or organization is changing and employees need to assess themselves and to think about their work differently;
- When there is high turnover and task simplicity; and
- When there are insufficient resources to support training.

Avoid using job aids in the following situations:

- When the credibility of the individual would be damaged;
- When it might be embarrassing to an individual to refer to other sources;
- When speedy reactions are essential;
- When novel and/or unpredictable situations are involved;
- When smooth, fluid, and masterful performance is a priority;
- When employees cannot read or cannot interpret visual displays;
- When employees are unaccustomed to consulting references; and
- When employees do not care about success.

Preview of Chapter 4

Chapter 4 introduces a key organizing concept for this book. There are three broad ways of talking about the uses of job aids: (1) to provide access to information; (2) to prompt procedures; and (3) to support better decision making. It is traditional to use job aids for the provision of information and procedures during performance. Chapter 4 makes a case for expanding the use of job aids to provide coaching and guidance for decisions.

References

Baine, D. (1986). *Memory and instruction.* Englewood Cliffs, NJ: Educational Technology Publications.

Brecke, F.H. (1982). Instructional design for aircrew judgment training. *Aviation, Space and Environmental Medicine, 53(10),* 951-957.

Clark, R.C. (1989). *Developing technical training.* Reading, MA: Addison-Wesley.

Clark, R.C. (1986). Part I: Task-general instructional methods, *Performance and Instruction, 25(3),17-21.*

Gagné, R.M., Briggs, L.J., & Wager, W.W. (1988). *Principles of instructional design.* New York: Holt, Rinehart and Winston.

Mandler, G. (1985). *Cognitive psychology: An essay in cognitive science.* Hillsdale, NJ: Lawrence Erlbaum Associates.

Minsky, M. (1985). *The society of mind.* New York: Simon & Schuster.

Kinds of Job Aids

Amy is in charge of mental-health services for a large jail. She supervises fifty full- and part-time counselors, psychologists, and social workers, who work in a situation in which there is frequent turnover. She recognizes that job aids have potential for orienting new employees and for relieving their constant reliance on her.

Alfonso is in charge of customer-service training for a computer software company. His company is demanding more skills and less training. He has always liked job aids and used them previously when he was training salespeople about products; he wonders if job aids could help in customer service, the softer side of the business.

Chapter 4 provides guidance for these and other professionals by supporting an expanded way of thinking about and using job aids that serve the following three functions:

1. Job aids that provide information;
2. Job aids that support procedures; and
3. Job aids that coach perspectives, decisions, and self-evaluation.

An Expanded View of Job Aids

This *Handbook* argues for a perspetive on job aids that includes and expands on the traditional one. What is traditional? What is the nature of an expanded view? Why should there be another and broader way of thinking about and using job aids? This introduction to Chapter 4 answers these questions.

Traditional Job Aids

Traditional job aids provide information or prompt procedures. Job aids typically enable job incumbents to access information and to carry out procedures when the information and procedures are unambiguous. Traditional job aids relieve the individual of responsibility for storing information and procedures in his or her long-term memory. When the information and procedures are stored in an external source—such as a computerized data base, a telephone book, or a pocket guide—the individual is responsible only for consulting and using that source.

Most job aids are used when the need arises rather than before or after the need arises. Traditional job aids are called on *during* performance, for example, when a pet owner needs to find a veterinarian who is available on Sunday, when a case worker must identify an attorney who speaks Swahili, when a teacher wants to thread a 16-millimeter projector, or when an operator wants to secure data in a computer.

A Broader View of Job Aids

A useful way to observe the shift in perspective on job aids is to focus on *what* job aids do and *when* they are used. Figure 4.1 outlines this change in focus.

	Traditional View	Expanded View
What Job Aids Do:	Provide information Support procedures	Provide information Support procedures Influence perspective and decision making
When Job Aids are Used:	During performance	During performance Prior to performance After performance

Figure 4.1. Traditional and Expanded Views of Job Aids

The traditional use of job aids is to help individuals to find relevant information (usually from large masses of information) and to execute procedures (often those that are complex or that have critical outcomes). However, job aids can do and be more. The following three broad applications exist for job aids:

1. To provide access to information;
2. To prompt procedures; and
3. To guide perspectives, decisions, and self-evaluation.

Although it is traditional to use job aids to help people access information and carry out procedures, the uses of job aids can be expanded to provide coaching and guidance for life's thornier challenges. Job aids can and should grow into support for writing, planning, managing, problem solving, and quality control.

Not only can job aids do more than previously thought; they also can be used on more occasions. Coaching job aids, for example, are not limited to use at the moment of challenge; they can be used five or ten or even thirty minutes prior to using the information that they convey. An example of this wider window of influence is the job aid that helps managers to manifest sensitivity to and congruence with equity guidelines while interviewing potential employees. Thirty minutes before the interview, a manager might review company policy, quotes from experts, and a checklist of things to keep in mind during the different phases of the interview. Consequently, the candidate sits down to a meeting with a more prepared and more confident manager. Although the job aid is nowhere in sight during the interview, its influence is felt.

Coaching and decision-making aids can improve performance *after* performance has occurred as well as before. They have potential for guiding and stimulating self-assessment, thereby enhancing the employee's ability to control the quality of the work. Joan Wackerman, of Wackerman Associates in Alexandria, Virginia, describes coaching job aids that enable instructional designers to examine their work critically before it reaches her or the client. Figure 4.2 is an example of one checklist she relies on to structure quality control. This coaching aid supports the development of instructor guides.

Foundations for a Broader View

In the early 1970s, job aids were influenced by behaviorism. Job aids helped people to hook up the cables and components of a ½-inch videotape system; they assisted people in all kinds of chores, such as changing the oil in a car, loading a dishwasher, and applying makeup.

LANGUAGE:

1. Easy to Read.
   - Use short sentences.
   - Use short paragraphs (two to four sentences per paragraph).
   - Use easy, short words.
   - Use the active voice.
   - Avoid jargon or acronyms.
   - Use subheadings liberally (three to five paragraphs per heading).

2. Bulleted, One-Line Information When Possible.
   - The first word after a bullet is capitalized; a period appears at the end of the sentence.
   - If the bulleted items are single words, use no capitalization and conclude them with commas.

CONSISTENCY OF HEADINGS AND TERMS:

   - INSTRUCTOR: Divide the class into groups....
   - TRANSITION: Explain that the next vugraph....
   - NOTE
   - POINT OUT
   - Example
   - Questions and Answers

STRUCTURE:

1. Guide should have an easily recognizable structure and substructure.
2. Consistent format highlighting (using either italics, bold, or underlining) for questions, examples, instructor comments.
3. One-to-one match with vugraph one-liners and instructor outline.
4. Enough detail that someone who is moderately familiar with the content can present it (that is, not too abbreviated).
5. Use of bullets, dashes, numbering, and lettering is consistent with the example provided.
   - Agreed-on hierarchy of bullets, dashes, and dots.
   - Agreed-on hierarchy of outline format.

Figure 4.2. Instructor Guide Development Checklist

In the 1980s, the Information Age emerged and people sought a broader conceptualization for job aids; as a result, job aids that provided access to information evolved. Personal calendars, telephone books, and computerized data bases came to be seen as having much in common with step-by-step guides to doing something. The concept of the job aid grew.

The definition of job aids continues to grow because of the influence of cognitive science. As learning psychology has shifted its orientation from behavioral to cognitive, the following new perspectives dominate:

1. A recognition of the importance of the individual's perspective on the quality of work;
2. A concern with the individual's self-perception and with readiness and confidence;
3. An eagerness for the individual to be conscious of how he or she is learning and organizing information;
4. An interest in how the individual thinks about, structures, and approaches a challenge; and
5. A belief that performance has roots in thoughts and speech.

No longer should people see job aids as simple stimuli that evoke an individual's response during the job. Job aids in the 1990s have the potential to influence the way people think and feel about themselves, their work, their co-workers, their managers, their clients, their problems, and their companies' products. A job aid that was submitted for a national award (Figure 4.3) illustrates this point. It had a column that was labeled "Why?" Managers were expected to provide reasons for the performance they were specifying for subordinates. Such a question would have been unheard of five or ten years ago.

As professionals attempt to make cognitive research useful in the workplace, job aids grow into tools that influence thoughts; feelings; and, eventually, effort and accomplishment. They do this by enhancing the visibility of the organization of

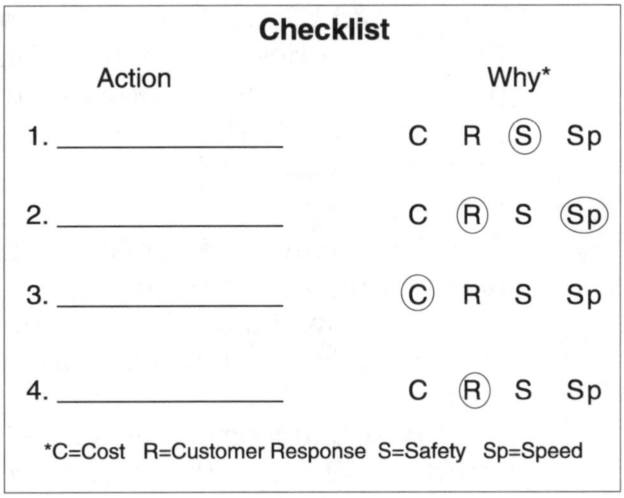

Figure 4.3. Checklist Job Aid That Addresses "Why"

subject matter, the mental models for approaching challenges, the perspectives on jobs, and the reasons for effort.

Demand for a Broader View

The following two examples illustrate the contrasting approaches to training and development:

> In the early 1980s, a large telecommunications company asked for assistance with a program to build the needs-assessment skills of course developers. A director said, "We want them to have a job aid for needs assessment, sort of a step-by-step approach, so they can't do it wrong."

> On the other hand, in the early 1990s, a manager from a government agency expressed a very different point of view by saying, "What we're looking for is a program that will alter the way our designers look at their jobs. We want them to see themselves as problem solvers, as consultants to their clients, with a responsibility for shaping the perspectives of the clients."

Businesses are no longer satisfied when employees manifest rote adherence to procedures. They seek out individuals who understand what they are doing and why they are doing it, so that they can adjust to unforeseen circumstances. These organizational changes are precipitating new approaches to training and development. Job aids, delivered through print and emergent technologies, can be potent tools in the employees' paradigm shifts toward increased access to information, processes, and choices.

Why Three Kinds of Job Aids?

The job-aid pie can be cut in many ways. This book proposes three categories of job aids based primarily on their purposes. Does the aid provide information? Does it support procedures? Or does it coach and encourage new perspectives and decisions?

Why These Three Kinds of Job Aids?

The three categories reflect a review of job aids from businesses and agencies across North America. Although there was some overlap and some combining of purposes, each aid was intended to influence information, procedures, or perspectives.

These categories respect historical, current, and future trends, including those that relate to technology. Training professionals have a history of relying on job aids to prompt procedures and to store and to make information accessible.

New job aids, delivered through technology and called expert systems and performance support tools (described in more detail in Chapter 11), have familiar applications and expand into coaching, advising, and supporting expanded perspectives.

Understanding the potential of all three kinds of job aids can stimulate new uses. A developer whose perception of job aids is limited to support for information or procedures will use them for that and only that. A wider view contributes to more opportunities for impact and cost savings.

In the sections that follow, the authors look at each of the three kinds of job aids in more detail, using the following general definition of job aids from Chapter 1:

> "A job aid is a repository for information, processes, or perspectives that is external to the individual and that supports work and activity by directing, guiding, and enlightening performance."

Job Aids for Informing

"Information" is one of the most bandied-about contemporary terms. There is "information overload," "information dump," "information anxiety," and "information bulimia." What these phrases share is a recognition of the explosion of information, the negative psychological effects of information profusion, and the human need to make sense of it all. The words that surround information establish a need for systems that diminish chaos, provide order, and support interaction with data. Informational job aids meet this need.

The quest for a definition for information is shown in Figure 4.4. It presents information as the key and stabilizing element between data and understanding. Wurman (1989) claims that data are not information until they have form and enable knowledge and understanding.

A job aid that informs is one that supports the individual by diminishing uncertainty. Informational job aids make data useful and become useful themselves when they meet the following criteria:

■ They form a stable repository for facts and concepts that answers the question of *who, what, which, when,* or *where;*

■ They are organized by user frame of reference, function, or subject-matter structure so as to emphasize relationships and connections;

■ They are accessible; and

■ They are actively employed by the user when they are needed.

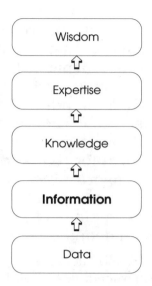

**Figure 4.4. The Role of Information
in an Information Society**

The following is a brief anecdote that illustrates a day in the life of a person who relies on informational job aids. Chapter 7, "Job Aids for Informing," provides detailed examples of such job aids, supported by developer commentaries.

Early in the morning, Terry turns to an informational job aid, Webster's Dictionary of the English Language, *to locate a dependable, non-anecdotal definition for the word "information."*

Over lunch, Terry decides to prepare for an upcoming trip to London and reaches for another informational job aid, London Access. *This guide is organized nontraditionally. In order to convert floods of data about London into useful information, the author made a calculated decision that visitors want information organized by geographical location; consequently, information in the guide is presented according to districts, areas, and places of interest in London. Only after the reader selects a district are the other meaningful categories of shops, galleries, parks, hotels, and so on presented. The author uses frequent and consistent summaries and color coding to reinforce meaning. The user enjoys easy access to information about which pubs and galleries are particularly interesting or enjoyable, which shops offer particular gifts, and where these places are in proximity to one another. The determination of which informa-tional aids to include was made on the basis of user needs and interests rather than by the inherent struc-ture of the subject matter.*

Later that same day, Terry uses a computerized data base, Knowledge Index, *to locate recent refer-ences for a review of the literature on the development of case studies.*

Just before bed, Terry decides to browse through Women's Outdoor Journal. *The journal is full of good ideas; for example, it includes a presentation of all the possible uses of a bandanna in the back country. In addition, this job aid provides step-by-step guidance for using the bandanna. Figure 4.5 illustrates this job aid, which represents a combination of informational job aids and those that support procedures.*

Job Aids for Supporting Procedures

In a complex and volatile world, in which many actions have potentially critical outcomes, individuals often turn to job aids to support them in carrying out a procedure. A proce-dure in this context is a prescribed way of doing something. Procedures mandate a particular course of action in a par-ticular sequence. Job aids that support procedures tell and show actions, order, and results.

Effective procedural job aids have the following charac-teristics in common:

- They answer the question "how";
- They answer the question "when";
- They emphasize *actions* by highlighting verbs;
- They present actions as steps, in order; and
- They often provide feedback, showing action paired with results, so that individuals can judge their effec-tiveness at each step as well as their effectivness for the entire procedure.

Two brief examples of procedural job aids follow. Chap-ter 8, "Job Aids for Procedures," provides more detailed ex-amples of procedural job aids along with commentaries by their developers.

NECK KERCHIEF
Fold in half diagonally, tie behind your neck. Keeps dust from sifting down your neck, sun off your neck, and makes a handy sweat wipe.

CAP
Fold in half diagonally, place on head with point of the V pointing down the back of your head. Tie ends behind your head, holding down the tip of the V. Keeps your hair clean, hair out of your eyes or out of the fire, and keeps bugs and spider webs out of your hair.

DUST BONNET
Put a knot in each corner of the bandanna to form a pocket in the middle to fit your head. Keeps the sun off your head and keeps hair clean. Dampen it to keep your head cool.

MASK
Fold in half diagonally, tie behind your neck (as in neck kerchief). Pull top of V over your nose. Filters out dust and pollen, keeps bugs off your face, warms bitingly cold winter air, and keeps you from being recognized during bank robberies.

HEADBAND
Fold or roll diagonally into a long strip about 1½ inches

wide. Place horizontally across forehead and tie behind the head. Keeps sweat from running into your eyes, keeps sweaty hair off your face, and generally makes you look cute.

SCARF
Fold in half diagonally. Place around neck with V to the back, tie in front of your throat. Keeps scratchy wool sweaters from scratching your neck, gives you that "sporty" look.

POUCH
Lay bandanna out flat. Place valuables in center. Tie opposite corners together with a square knot. Carry by the knots or slip a pole, hobo fashion, between the two knots and carry it over your shoulder.

BIB
Holding bandanna flat across your chest, tie adjacent corners behind your neck. Keeps drippy food off your clothes.

BREAD COZY
Lay bandanna in basket or pot. Place bread in center and bring corners up and over the bread, keeping it warm.

PLACEMAT
Eating on the ground or off a

rock? Spread a handkerchief down as a placemat. It adds a festive look to ordinary picnics.

NAPKINS
Fold a bandanna into a rectangle and lay beside your supper bowl. It adds color and lets everyone know you have breeding.

FOOD COVER
Spread a bandanna over food to keep the flies or bugs off.

POT HOLDER
Fold or wad the bandanna into several thicknesses and use to grasp hot pots.

SEAT SAVER
Spread a bandanna on ground or picnic table before sitting down to keep dirt or grass stains off clothing.

BUG REPELLER
Save sensitive skin from harsh insect repellents. Spray or moisten bandanna with bug dope and tie around neck, wrists, or ankles.

BERRY BAG
Fold bandanna lengthwise into a rope. Tie a knot in each end. Spread out space between the knots to form a pouch.

STRAINER
Make berry bag (above) and fill with fruit. Pour water over the fruit, letting it drain through the cloth.

APRON
Tuck one side of bandanna into waistband of pants. Let rest of bandanna hang down to protect clothing.

TABLECLOTH
Want to spruce up a rock or picnic table for an intimate outdoor dinner? Spread bandanna diagonally between the two guests.

NAPKINS
Fold or knot bandannas into fancy shapes to accompany tablecloth for that fancy feast.

CUFF TIGHTENER
Tie pants cuffs close to your ankles to keep floppy pant legs from getting in bicycle chains or becoming trip hazards.

BANDAGE
Hold gauze bandage in place, cover a wound, or support sprained wrist or ankle by wrapping bandanna around the injury. Fold diagonally in a 1½- to 2-inch-wide strip and tie in place.

SPLINT
Fold bandanna diagonally into a narrow strip. Immobilize broken limb by tying it to a straight tree branch.

ROPE
Twist bandanna diagonally to make a strong tie.

FLAG
Mark a spot by tying a bandanna to a tree branch. Bright colors make it easy to spot.

WASHCLOTH
Lather yourself with a soap-filled bandanna. It rinses easily, dries quickly, and washes bandanna in the process.

TOWEL
Absorbent cotton bandannas soak up water quickly.

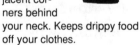

Figure 4.5. Combination Job Aid Showing Possible Uses of a Bandanna

Example 1. Many computer products, especially telecommunications programs, seem maddeningly idiosyncratic. Steve Wagner-Davis, designer of interactive videodisks at the University of California, constructed the procedural job aid shown in Figure 4.6 for accessing a certain computerized data base.

1. Set software and modem to FULL duplex.
2. Set software to 1200 baud rate.
3. Under FILE MENU, set software to capture incoming data to text file.
4. Dial 233-0323 and press ENTER.
5. System Prompt: Modem connected.
   Your Response: Press ENTER twice.
6. System Prompt: Terminal=
   Your Response: Type D1

**Figure 4.6. Procedural Job Aid
for Accessing a Computerized Data Base**

Example 2. Michael Wolfe, a graduate student in Educational Technology at San Diego State University and an avionics engineer at General Dynamics, illustrates in Figure 4.7 the importance of a clear display of action steps paired with the results of action. Note how key actions and feedback are emphasized.

Examples of procedural job aids are common. For example, procedural job aids include the documentation that supports computer hardware and software and the booklet that accompanies a car or a videocassette recorder. On kitchen shelves, job aids can be found on bottles of sauce, bags of pasta, and in every cookbook.

Job Aids for Coaching Perspectives and Supporting Decisions

Although most procedural job aids draw on algorithms, coaching aids offer a useful heuristic for approaching and evaluating tasks. Algorithms, as defined by Rossett (1987), are clear, unvarying steps in an order that handles a narrow class of problems. Most current computer programs represent algorithms; their steps, order, decisions, alternatives, and results are known and concrete. The process of taking money out of an automatic-teller machine, ascertaining interest payments on an automobile loan payment, or putting gas in a car are three examples of algorithms.

Heuristics, on the other hand, suggest ways to think about the ambiguous areas of life and work. Heuristics pro-

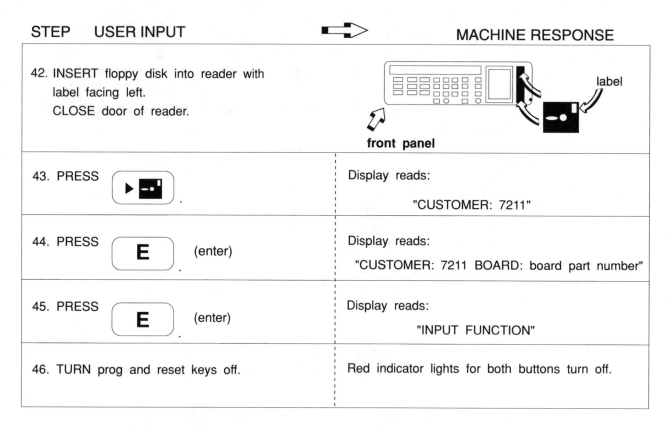

Figure 4.7. Procedural Job Aid Showing Key Actions and Feedback

vide guidelines for topics that plunge people into "gray areas," questions and problems that lack straightforward answers. In place of the comfort of steps are rules of thumb that can be considered before, during, or after the challenge.

Although algorithms set out an ordered and clear path, heuristics are built for life's thornier problems. For example, heuristics come into play when someone is figuring out whether or not to borrow money to buy an automobile, preparing to interview a potential employee, or getting ready to make a public presentation. Algorithms, as described in the procedures section previously, are neatly presented in numbered lists or boxes with arrows.

Heuristics are most often represented as bulleted relationships, in which each bullet suggests an idea, question, or topic worthy of consideration. Algorithms tell individuals what to do and in what order. Heuristics encourage people to think about things in a particular way, leaving open the possibility that the order will vary and that items will be emphasized, omitted, or added. Algorithms lead naturally to procedural job aids; heuristics produce coaching job aids that guide perspectives and decisions.

Effective coaching job aids have many of the following characteristics:

- They answer the question "why";
- They answer the question "how," as in "How might I think about or approach that?";
- They allow for uncertainty and encourage discussion about confidence levels;
- They make suggestions rather than provide directions;
- They emphasize thoughts, feelings, and meanings;
- They model organization and perspectives on work and life;
- They articulate quality standards;
- They encourage a dialog with the user, especially a dialog about reasons, feelings, and approaches; and
- They encourage interaction with the job aid, pressing the individual to add or highlight guidelines.

A story about Albert Einstein (Schramm & Porter, 1982) is appropriate to this discussion. When asked a question about the single event most helpful in developing the theory of relativity, Einstein reportedly responded, "Figuring out how to think about the problem."

Two brief examples of coaching job aids follow. Chapter 9, "Job Aids for Decision Making and Coaching," provides more detailed examples of coaching job aids along with commentaries by their developers.

Example 1. Marcella Ruch, a weight-loss consultant, developed the following job aid to advise people on how to alter their homes to support weight loss:

- Is a jug of water readily available?
- Have foods on the forbidden list been removed from the house or placed out of sight?
- Is an airtight container of cut vegetables in easy reach?
- Are diet salad dressings and low-calorie snacks in easy reach?
- Are nonalcoholic beverages, such as mineral water and club soda, available and cold?

Certainly this checklist could be portrayed as an algorithm, as steps to success. However, the list is more accurately a heuristic, because the order of activity is not critical to success. What counts is considering and moving forward on these rules of thumb, as well as tailoring them to the individual's situation. This heuristic aid, like the Instructor Guide Development Checklist presented as Figure 4.2, encourages the user to monitor himself or herself with particular standards in mind.

Example 2. Coaching or heuristic aids can also guide a particular approach to a challenge. For example, United Van Lines distributes a brochure to assist people in doing their own packing for moving. They provide checklists to remind movers of the bases that must be covered as part of an effective move. Planning ahead, for example, includes gathering the following items:

- Various sizes of sturdy cartons with lids (flaps) that can be completely closed;
- White paper, tissue paper, paper toweling, or newsprint—good for all-purpose wrapping and cushioning;
- Gummed tape and/or strong twine for sealing packed cartons;
- Scissors and/or sharp knives (keep them out of the reach of children);
- Felt markers for labeling cartons; and
- A notebook and pencil for listing cartons as they are packed.

Also included in the brochure is a quality checklist, whose first item includes a reason. Good packing, according to United Van Lines, means taking the following actions:

- Limiting cartons, where possible, to a maximum weight of fifty pounds to make handling easier;
- Wrapping items carefully; and
- Providing plenty of cushioning to absorb shock.

Revisiting Amy and Alfonso

This chapter opened with the challenges of two professionals. The following suggestions could be made for their particular situations:

Amy, the manager of mental-health workers at a large jail, could use informational aids to help her colleagues to learn where to find what they need. Numerous county and organizational resources provide services to inmates before and during the trial process. Employees seek two levels of information support: (1) a comprehensive source, either printed or computerized, that is organized by need or function and that is readily available in the counseling and treatment area; and (2) a portable, abbreviated pocket guide that answers questions most frequently encountered when professionals are seeing inmates in many locations throughout the jail.

Amy also needs to provide new employees with an algorithm that represents the flow of events and procedures for their clients. As Schmid and Gerlach (1990) suggest, there is value in serializing and representing information in ordered and sparse detail.

However, the majority of the important challenges facing mental-health employees have no easy answers. For example, Amy's people often must make tough decisions about whether or not to put people in isolation, whether someone is serious about a threat of suicide, and whether to request consultation from a psychiatrist or support from an armed guard. Amy should consider collaborating with experienced staff members to develop coaching aids that will provide professionals with a series of questions and guidelines to prepare them for critical situations.

Alfonso, a training manager for a computer software company, has a history of reliance on information and procedural aids for sales training. In fact, his first effort when he got the new position in customer service was to write out procedural steps for handling a customer complaint. Unfortunately, although it looked good, it did not solve the problems. Customer-service representatives claimed that they could not follow all the steps in the heated interaction of the moment.

Alfonso decided to use a heuristic job aid to influence the way these people approached customers. He began by assembling a group of people he considered to be effective representatives and asked them about recurring challenges. Eventually he came up with five general problems. He then asked the selected representatives how they would approach these challenges. He wanted to know what they did, what they thought about as they did it, why they did it, and what made it work. Alfonso then prepared a coaching aid that captured and conveyed these perspectives and guidelines for this inner game of customer service.

Review of Chapter 4

Traditional job aids serve the following purposes:

- To provide information;

- To prompt procedures; and
- To be useful at the time of the challenge.

In an expanded view, job aids serve these purposes:

- To provide information;
- To prompt procedures;
- To coach perspectives and decisions; and
- To be useful before, during, and after challenges.

It is important to expand the view for the following reasons:

- Cognitive psychology;
- Changes in organizations; and
- Market demand.

Job aids to inform share the following characteristics:

- They answer the question of "who," "what," "where," "when," or "which"; and
- They make answers accessible.

Job aids for procedures share the following characteristics:

- They answer "how" and "when"; and
- They show steps in order.

Job aids for decisions share the following characteristics:

- They answer "why" and "how do I think about it";
- They make suggestions about approaches;
- They emphasize thoughts and feelings;
- They address ambiguities; and
- They articulate standards for quality.

Preview of Chapter 5

Chapter 5 presents six job-aid formats and matches these formats with appropriate media. It answers questions about which format is best in a particular situation and what means of delivery are available.

References

Clark, R.C. (1989). *Developing technical training.* Reading, MA: Addison-Wesley.

Rossett, A. (1987). *Training needs assessment.* Englewood Cliffs, NJ: Educational Technology Publications.

Schmid, R.F., & Gerlach, V.S. (1990). Instructional design rules for algorithmic subject matter. *Performance Improvement Quarterly, 3*(2), 1-14.

Schramm, W., & Porter, W. (1982). *Men, women, messages and media: Understanding human communication* (2nd ed.). New York: Harper & Row.

Wurman, R.S. (1987). *London access.* New York: Access Press.

Wurman, R.S. (1989). *Information anxiety.* New York: Doubleday.

Zagorksi, S. (1987). How I created the award-winning job aid. *Performance and Instruction, 26*(4), 29-32.

Zuboff, S. (1988). *In the age of the smart machine: The future of work and power.* New York: Basic Books.

Part Two

Developing Job Aids

Formats for Job Aids

Ruth, the supervisor of training for a utility company, is trying to decide how to format her job aids. What are her options?

How can Marianne, a training manager for a large hotel chain, help personnel clerks to distribute the correct employee-benefits brochures when there are nine different versions?

How might Jorge develop job aids for workers who are restricted from using "printed" or "paper" job aids because they do their jobs with their eyes on the road?

Chapter 5 provides guidance for these and other professionals by answering the following three questions:

1. From what formats may designers choose?
2. Which format is best for a particular situation?
3. What means are available to deliver job aids?

From What Formats May Designers Choose?

The job-aid format determines how information is presented to the user. Harless (1988) developed a lean and effective way to classify formats, which has been adapted and expanded in this chapter. The following seven formats for job aids are possible:

1. Steps;
2. Work sheets;
3. Arrays;
4. Decision tables;
5. Flow charts;
6. Checklists; and
7. Combinations.

In the following sections, each of the seven formats is described and is illustrated briefly. Chapters 7, 8, and 9 provide opportunities to view job aids more comprehensively by looking at several examples and commentaries.

Steps

The step format, as its name suggests, presents information, directions, and activities in sequence. When a developer selects the step format, he or she wants to ensure a flow of actions, in a particular order, for a narrowly defined purpose. Step job aids include numbers, verbs, and objects that often appear as a procedure manual, a "to-do" list, or a computer help screen. A major attribute of the step format is that no complex decisions or written responses are expected of the user.

Figure 5.1 shows a portion of a job aid that was developed to help new computer users at the Army Logistics Management College turn on their machines and access a particular main menu.

When a job aid requires the user to do trivial tasks, like checking or filling in a copied number, and when the detail and order are critical, the step format is appropriate. The main purpose of a step job aid is to guide the user through sequential steps.

Figure 5.2 shows a job aid that was developed to show district accountants how to process a work order. The emphasis is on the sequence of steps for processing a work order rather than on completing the information.

Work Sheets

The work-sheet format is also characterized by steps that must be performed in sequence. In addition, work sheets require the user to participate in substantive written responses, usually in the form of calculations.

The main purpose of the work sheet is to generate the result of the calculations, enabling the individual to find out how much is owed to the government, how much pesticide to

TO TURN ON THE MACHINE AND ACCESS AMCISS MAIN MENU

Now that you're sitting at your terminal work station ready to go, you have realized that before you can use AMCISS you must get to it. The way to do that is to turn on your machine and then access the AMCISS main menu. Following these steps will get you there with ease:

STEP 1. Press the "on" switch located on the front-right side of the terminal. The screen will be blank, with the cursor in the upper-left corner.

STEP 2. Then press

> Return

.

This message will be on your screen:

```
- - - - - - - - Welcome to KEEnet - - - - - - -
D01.15 - - - - - - - - - - - - - - - - - 870310
PIU Network Address: 3425 Port: C
Current Device Name: 3425C
- - - - - - - - - - - - - - - - - - - - - - - - - -
```

Figure 5.1. Step Job Aid for Turning on the Machine and Accessing AMCISS Main Menu

STEP	ACTION
1.	Assign the work order a number from the Work Order Log Book. Work Order Log: Number 236, Start Date 6–18, Completion Date 8–24; 237 — Assign Next Number
2.	File white copy on pending file by date. work order ➜ pending file (DATE)
3.	Give pink copy to foreman.
4.	When foreman returns copy, log in completion date in Work Order Log. Work Order Log: Number 236, Start Date 6–18, Completion Date 8–24; 237, Start Date 6–25

Figure 5.2. Step Job Aid for Processing a Work Order

spray on a lawn, or who is eligible for a home loan. Work sheets are often presented as forms or applications for which the users must read instructions, provide information, and complete calculations.

Figure 5.3 shows a portion of a work-sheet job aid developed to help account managers at General Motors to determine approximate or reasonable costs for the evaluation portion of a training program.

Figure 5.4 shows a portion of a work-sheet job aid developed by Roger Addison at Wells Fargo Bank, which provides more embedded information than the previous example. Support is provided to the employee whose task it is to determine and to justify production costs.

Arrays

Arrays present bodies of information with meaningful organization and structure. This format allows the user to access large bodies of data, generally to support the completion of a larger job or task. The user of a job aid in an array format is attempting to answer one of three questions: who, what, or where. The user starts with a clearly defined need, such as finding out the zip code for Hutchinson, Kansas, and then refers to an array to find the answer. For instance, an author would refer to a word array, or dictionary, to ensure that words are spelled correctly. The array may be in the form of a conventional dictionary or an automated spelling checker. In another case, a social worker might refer to an array job

F. Evaluation	Costs
1. Client meeting. $\_\_\_\_\_$ /hr x_____hrs. =	
2. Sample target population. $\_\_\_$ /hr. x ___ hrs =	
3. Develop instruments. $\_\_\_$ /hr. x ___ hrs x ___ instruments =	
4. Client review. No charge	
5. Implement evaluation. $\_\_\_$ /hr. x ___ hrs =	
6. Evaluate data/write report. $\_\_\_$ /hr. x ___ hrs =	
7. Submit report. No charge	
F. *Total cost of evaluation =*	

Figure 5.3. Work-Sheet Job Aid for Calculating Evaluation Costs

COST JUSTIFICATION WORK SHEET   Project _____   Svc. Mgr. _____

CURRENT COST

1. Calculate labor costs for each employee:

Emp #1
HRS/WK ON TASK   = ___ A
HOURLY SALARY   =$ ___ B
BENEFITS @ 30%   =$ ___ C
A x [B+ C] x 52 WKS   =$ ___ D

Emp #2
HRS/WK ON TASK   = ___ A
HOURLY SALARY   =$ ___ B
BENEFITS @ 30%   =$ ___ C
A x [B+C] x 52 WKS   =$ ___ D

ADD ALL D's TO CALCULATE
TOTAL ANNUAL LABOR $ ___ E

2. Calculate supplies cost for all supplies used in the task that must be replaced. Do not calculate if current proposed costs are the same:

ITEM #1
QUANTITY USED/WK   =$ ___ A
ITEM COST   =$ ___ B
A x B x 52 WKS   =$ ___ C

ITEM #2
QUANTITY USED/WK   =$ ___ A
ITEM COST   =$ ___ B
A x B x 52 WKS   =$ ___ C

TOTAL ANNUAL SUPPLIES $ ___ E

3. Calculate cost of equipment rental, lease, and maintenance only if equipment will not be used in proposed costs:

ITEM #1
ANNUAL COST $ ___ A

ITEM #2
ANNUAL COST $ ___ A

TOTAL ANNUAL EQUIP/MAINT $ ___ G

PROPOSED COST (AFTER)

1. Calculate proposed labor costs:

Emp #1
HRS/WK ON TASK   = ___ A
HOURLY SALARY   =$ ___ B
BENEFITS @ 30%   =$ ___ C
A x [B+C] x 52 WKS   =$ ___ D

Emp #2
HRS/WK ON TASK   = ___ A
HOURLY SALARY   =$ ___ B
BENEFITS @ 30%   =$ ___ C
A x [B+C] x 52 WKS   =$ ___ D

ADD ALL D's TO CALCULATE
TOTAL ANNUAL LABOR $ ___ E

2. Calculate proposed supplies cost:

ITEM #1
QUANTITY USED/WK   =$ ___ A
ITEM COST   =$ ___ B
A x B x 52 WKS   =$ ___ C

ITEM #2
QUANTITY USED/WK   =$ ___ A
ITEM COST   =$ ___ B
A x B x 52 WKS   =$ ___ C

TOTAL ANNUAL SUPPLIES $ ___ E

3. Calculate proposed equipment cost:

ITEM #1
ANNUAL COST $ ___ A

ITEM #2
ANNUAL COST $ ___ A

TOTAL ANNUAL EQUIP/MAINT $ ___ G

CURRENT COST(BEFORE)

4. Calculate operating costs for items such as postage, rent, utilities, computer time, cross-charges:

ITEM #1
WEEKLY USAGE   =$ ___ A
ITEM COST   =$ ___ B
A x B x 52 WKS   =$ ___ C

ITEM #2
WEEKLY USAGE   =$ ___ A
ITEM COST   =$ ___ B
A x B x 52 WKS   =$ ___ C

TOTAL ANNUAL SUPPLIES $ ___ E

6. Total current costs:
Add all the E Figures:
TOTAL ANNUAL LABOR $ ___
TOTAL ANNUAL SUPPLIES $ ___
TOTAL ANNUAL EQUIP. $ ___
TOTAL ANNUAL OPER. $ ___

TOTAL CURRENT COSTS: $ ___ F

7. ANNUAL NET SAVINGS
Calculate the difference between the current and proposed total costs:
F   =$ ___
H   =$ ___

F minus H   =$ ___   Annual Net Savings

Determine hard and soft dollar costs:
Hard $ savings   =$ ___
Soft $ savings   =$ ___

PROPOSED COST (AFTER)

4. Calculate proposed operating costs:

ITEM #1
WEEKLY USAGE   =$ ___ A
ITEM COST   =$ ___ B
A x B x 52 WKS   =$ ___ C

ITEM #2
WEEKLY USAGE   =$ ___ A
ITEM COST   =$ ___ B
A x B x 52 WKS   =$ ___ C

TOTAL ANNUAL SUPPLIES $ ___ G

5. Calculate one-time costs for construction, moving, and new equipment:

ITEM #1
ONE-TIME COST $ ___ A

ITEM #2
ONE-TIME COST $ ___ A

TOTAL ONE-TIME COST $ ___ G

6. Total proposed costs:
Add all the G Figures:
TOTAL ANNUAL LABOR $ ___
TOTAL ANNUAL SUPPLIES $ ___
TOTAL ANNUAL EQUIP. $ ___
TOTAL ANNUAL OPER. $ ___
TOTAL ONE-TIME COSTS $ ___

TOTAL PROPOSED COSTS $ ___ H

Figure 5.4. Job Aid for Justifying Costs

aid to find places in Los Angeles County that provide health services in the Tagalog language for Filipino clients.

The job aid in Figure 5.5 was designed to provide a reference for Automated Clearing House (ACH) department employees to use when changing account information. In order to change a piece of information in the computer system, the ACH employee must enter the correct code.

This array job aid was developed to communicate new codes. It will become unnecessary, as often happens with job aids, because the employees use the twelve codes frequently. Array aids are particularly useful when the amount of data is great or changes frequently.

Decision Tables

Decision tables represent "if-then" situations. This format allows the user to identify solutions for given problems based on the conditions of the situation. A decision table is used

---

CHANGE CODES:

C01 -   INCORRECT ACCOUNT NUMBER - CCD, CTP, PPD

C02 -   INCORRECT TRANSIT ROUTING NUMBER - CCD, CTP, PPD

C03 -   INCORRECT T/R NUMBER AND INCORRECT ACCOUNT NUMBER - CCD, CTP, PPD

C04 -   ACCOUNT NAME CHANGE - CCD, CTP, PPD

C05 -   INCORRECT TRANSACTION CODE - PPD

C06 -   INCORRECT ACCOUNT NUMBER - CIE, MTE

C07 -   INCORRECT TRANSIT ROUTING NUMBER - CIE, MTE

C08 -   INCORRECT T/R NUMBER AND INCORRECT ACCOUNT NUMBER - CIE, MTE

C09 -   INCORRECT INDIVIDUAL IDENTIFICATION NUMBER - CIE, MTE

C10 -   INCORRECT COMPANY NAME - CIE, MTE

C11 -   INCORRECT COMPANY IDENTIFICATION

C12 -   INCORRECT COMPANY NAME AND COMPANY IDENTIFICATION - CIE, MTE

Figure 5.5. Array Job Aid for Changing Account Information

when the problem includes several conditions that influence the selection of the correct answer or action.

Marianne, the hotel training manager mentioned at the beginning of this chapter, developed the example shown in Figure 5.6 to provide an easy way for personnel clerks to identify the appropriate benefits brochures to give employees.

To use the decision table in Figure 5.6, the user needs little or no background. In other instances, the user must be knowledgeable about the job or task to be able to distinguish between the choices. Judith Hale of Hale Associates provides the example shown in Figure 5.7. This decision table enables a committee chairperson to lead a meeting and to comply with parliamentary procedure.

Figure 5.7 is an example of a lean "if-then" matrix. In prose, the description of an action becomes cumbersome: If the "Action" is "Fix the time at which to adjourn," then the board must "Second"; no one may "Debate"; the board may "Amend" the action, but only with a "Majority" vote; it may "Reconsider"; and no one may "Interrupt." A decision table renders this challenge as easy as running a finger down a column and across a row.

Department	Hourly Employee	Benefits Brochure No.
Maintenance	Yes	123
	No	50
Housekeeping	Yes	136
	No	52
Food Service	Yes	148
	No	53
Sales	Yes	152
	No	54

**Figure 5.6. Decision-Table Job Aid for
Choosing a Benefits Brochure**

Action	Second	Debate	Amend	Vote	Reconsider	Interrupt
Fix time at which to adjourn	Yes	No	Yes	Maj.	Yes	No
Adjourn	Yes	No	No	Maj.	No	No
Recess	Yes	No	Yes	Maj.	No	No

Figure 5.7. Decision-Table Job Aid for Reviewing Parliamentary Procedures

General Telephone and Electronics (GTE) uses the decision-table format in an extensive series of job aids to support engineers in the consistent determination of cost, labor, and maintenance provisions for laying cable. Figure 5.8 illustrates a portion of a six-page job aid.

Decision tables may stand alone or may depend heavily on trained users and other supports. The benefits-brochure job aid (Figure 5.6) provides all the information needed to distribute the appropriate brochure. The user needs only to know where the brochures are stored. The parliamentary-procedure job aid (Figure 5.7) requires the user to have command of the possible range of meeting actions. Beyond that, a novice parliamentarian can use it with ease. The GTE-engineering job aid (Figure 5.8) is part of a larger performance system that is supported by additional job aids; it exists to support experienced users.

Flow Charts

The flow-chart format is a sequence of questions that can be answered with "yes" or "no." Once the user answers "yes" or

Is It	Will Line Density Be	Rule 34 Calls It	Then
Mining, Drilling, Campaign, or Promotional	⟶	Speculative	Apply Rule 35
Service for 12 Months or Less	⟶	Temporary	GO
Planned Development or Mobile Home Park with 5 or More Lots	5 or More Nontemporary Lines with at least 1 Line per Acre (see note)	Subdivision	TO
			TABLE
Planned Development or Trailer Park with 5 or More Lots	Fewer than 5 lines, or Less than 1 Line per Acre	Real Estate Development	C
4 or Fewer Residential Lots, or	⟶	Other Applicant	
4 or Fewer Dwellings in one or more buildings on a single parcel, or			
5 or More Dwellings in a single building on a single parcel, or			
One Enterprise on a single or continuous parcel of land			

Figure 5.8. Decision-Table Job Aid for Determining Development Type

"no," an appropriate path to the next decision is indicated. The performer follows the question path until enough information is gathered to reach a conclusive end.

The flow-chart format, like the decision-table format, guides a user through a decision-making process. They differ in that the flow-chart format is used for binary questions, those for which the answer to the question is "yes" or "no," thus leading the user to one path or another.

Figure 5.9 is a Wells Fargo Bank flow chart that was created to help training managers to determine whether to seek an outside contractor.

Checklists

Like most job aids, the checklist format enables the user not to rely on memory. This format is distinct, however, in that its main purpose is to prompt the user to think about things in a certain way. Checklist job aids are often used to list critical information that the user must consider or verify before, during, or after performing a job or task.

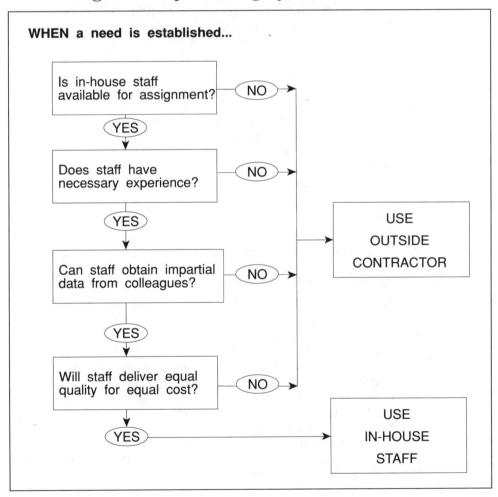

Figure 5.9. Flow-Chart Job Aid for Selecting Contractors

The checklist job aid presents heuristics. As stated previously, heuristics are considerations, guidelines, and rules of thumb that enlighten performance. They offer ways of approaching topics, issues, and problems. Healthy people may have heuristics for selecting the foods they eat each day; wealthy people may have effective heuristics for selecting investments; and wise people allow experiences to alter their heuristics. For example, a person may have a heuristic that helps to decide whether or not there is time to exercise in the morning. However, if just once that person decides to squeeze in a jog—despite an 8:00 a.m. meeting—and it works out well, then that person is likely to alter the heuristic, the guideline used to make decisions about the topic.

As George Geis (1984) contends, the checklist format presents a series of statements that describes critical attributes. They can be the attributes of a good used car, issues to consider when selecting produce for a large and special dinner party, or things to keep in mind when preparing to make a public presentation. Figure 5.10, "The Questionnaire Writer's Checklist" from *Training Needs Assessment* (Rossett, 1987),

The cover
- ☐ Purpose
- ☐ Direct address
- ☐ Appropriate words for audience
- ☐ How selected to receive survey
- ☐ Reason for responding
- ☐ How and when to respond
- ☐ Expression of appreciation

The directions
- ☐ Brief
- ☐ Clear
- ☐ Appropriate to the audience
- ☐ Defining when necessary
- ☐ Providing examples when necessary

The items
- ☐ One purpose per item
- ☐ Each item linked to an item type
- ☐ Primarily forced-choice items
- ☐ Reliance on combinational items to include open-ended option
- ☐ Appropriate use of highlighting, underlining, and white space
- ☐ Consistency in scales and question type
- ☐ Content clustering by meaningful portions of the job or task
- ☐ Numbered items and pages
- ☐ Words and sentences appropriate to reading level and interests
- ☐ Communication with data-processing professional, if appropriate
- ☐ Sufficient testing to revise and feel confident

Figure 5.10. Checklist Job Aid for Writing Questionnaires

helps writers to structure their thought processes as they prepare surveys. It provides a comprehensive listing of the arenas that survey planners must pose, ponder, resolve, and incorporate. The checklist is useful before planners write surveys, while they puzzle over them, and after they complete the drafts.

Figure 5.11 is another example of a checklist job aid. An assistant in an automobile repair shop uses this format to provide information to the mechanic, speeding up the diagnostic process and allowing the repair shop to begin repairs with the labor of lower-paid employees. The mechanic then uses this information as a starting point.

The vehicle diagnostic checklist illustrates how checklist job aids usually do not produce a single answer. What they do is influence the determination and consideration of an array of approaches.

Checklists are commonly used to improve consistency and reliability. The checklist shown in Figure 5.12, developed by Aida Pasigna and Sivasailam Thiagarajan, helps writers to review their work to ensure that simple language

---

1. Describe what happened before your car died.

2. Has this happened before? If so, describe when and what happened.

3. When you turn the key, how does the car respond? (Check one)

    ☐   It turns over but does not start.

    ☐   At first is turns over; then it seems to wind down, and then it doesn't turn over at all.

    ☐   I hear a clicking sound but the car does not turn over.

    ☐   Nothing.

    ☐   Other (please describe below).

4. Do your lights work?

Figure 5.11. Checklist Job Aid for Vehicle Diagnostics

A. WORDS

1. Length. *Words are short and simple.*
2. Familiarity of Proper Nouns. *Proper nouns are well known, short, and easy to pronounce.*
3. Clarity of Antecedents. *All of the pronouns have clear antecedents.*
4. Use of Technical Terms. *Technical terms are used only when they form an essential part of the concept or information taught.*
5. Definition of Technical Terms. *Technical terms are defined first before they are used.*
6. Use of Examples/Nonexamples. *Examples and nonexamples are used for defining technical terms.*
7. Special Meanings. *If a common word is used to refer to a special meaning, the special meaning is defined before the word is used in that context.*
8. Noun and Verb Forms. *Verb forms are clearly distinct from the nouns.*
9. Critical Adjectives. *Critical adjectives have been emphasized.*
10. Idiomatic Usage. *Idiomatic expressions and complex verb phrases (e.g., verb-plus-preposition constructions such as "called up" or "put up with") have been avoided unless they constitute part of the teaching information and are taught first before they are used.*
11. Complex Verb Phrases. *Auxiliary verbs, such as "could," "might," and "does," have been avoided in constructions such as "He does know how to read."*

**Figure 5.12. Checklist Job Aid for Writing for People
with Limited English Proficiency**

is used when writing for people whose primary language is not English.

Combination Job Aids

The formats mentioned previously may be combined. For example, an operating-room attendant needs to follow a strict series of steps for preparing the operating room for a particular procedure that is performed infrequently. One of the steps on the list might be "Check that all surgical instruments are on the surgeon's tray." If many instruments are required, the job aid might include a separate checklist for ensuring that each instrument has been accounted for.

The United States Federal Tax Form is another example of a combination job aid. The primary format used for the 1040 form is a work sheet. The guidelines that accompany the 1040 are in a step format. However, when the steps become complex because decisions must be made, other formats (such as decision tables, flow charts, and checklists) are used. For example, the flow chart in Figure 5.13 helps taxpayers to determine whether or not a dependent is legally bound to file a tax return. Figure 5.14 presents supporting steps in completing the tax return, which include brief directions and examples. The decision table shown in Figure 5.15 helps the user to determine just how much is owed in taxes.

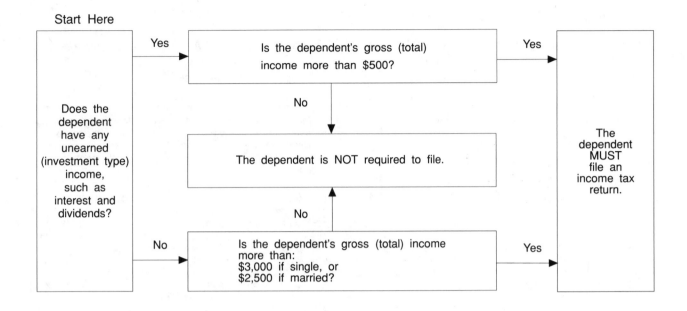

**Figure 5.13. Flow-Chart Job Aid for Determining
if a Dependent Must File a Tax Return**

**Step 1 - Name, Address,
and Social Security Number**

Don and Jean use the label that came with their forms package. The label has their names, addresses, and social security numbers. They check the label to make sure it is correct, but they do not put it on the return until they have completed and checked the return to make sure it is accurate. If they use the label, their tax return can be processed faster.

The Smiths should use the label even if some of the information on it is incorrect. They would make any necessary changes directly on the label.

Presidential Election Campaign Fund. Don and Jean each want $1 of their taxes to go to this fund. They check both "Yes" boxes. Checking "Yes" does not increase their tax or reduce their refund.

Step 2 - Filing Status

Don and Jean must choose their filing status before they figure their tax liability.

Filing status (lines 1-5). Don and Jean check the box on line 2 to file a joint return. Because they are married and living together they must file a joint return in order to claim the child-care credit.

Step 3 - Exemptions

Don and Jean must indicate the number of exemptions they can claim.

Exemptions (lines 6a-e). Don and Jean can take two personal exemptions, one for each of them. They check these exemptions in the boxes on lines 6a and 6b and enter the total (2) on the line at the right. On line 6c, they write their children's names and enter "2" on the line at the right.

Figure 5.14. Step Job Aid for Completing Tax Return

If line 7 (1040EZ), line 19 (1040A), or line 37 (1040) is—		And you are —				If line 7 (1040EZ), line 19 (1040A), or line 37 (1040) is—		And you are—				If line 7 (1040EZ), line 19 (1040A), or line 37 (1040) is—		And you are—			
At least	But less than	Single	Married filing jointly	Married filing separately	Head of household	At least	But less than	Single	Married filing jointly	Married filing separately	Head of household	At least	But less than	Single	Married filing jointly	Married filing separately	Head of household
		Your tax is—						Your tax is—						Your tax is—			
$0	$5	$0	$0	$0	$0	1,400	1,425	212	212	212	212	2,700	2,725	407	407	407	407
5	15	2	2	2	2	1,425	1,450	216	216	216	216	2,725	2,750	411	411	411	411
15	25	3	3	3	3	1,450	1,475	219	219	219	219	2,750	2,775	414	414	414	414
25	50	6	6	6	6	1,475	1,500	223	223	223	223	2,775	2,800	418	418	418	418
50	75	9	9	9	9	1,500	1,525	227	227	227	227	2,800	2,825	422	422	422	422
75	100	13	13	13	13	1,525	1,550	231	231	231	231	2,825	2,875	426	426	426	426

Figure 5.15. Array Job Aid for Determining the Amount of Tax Owed

STEPS:	SYSTEM RESPONSE:
6. If the traffic direction (worksheet item #4) | IS	THEN GO TO:
Incoming	Step 7
Outgoing	
Bi-directional	Step 11:		
7. Type: y	Enter port name you want to modify [q]:
8. Enter the second port name (worksheet item #7)	Do you want port... Enter 1 incoming 2 outgoing 3 bi-directional (default remains the same):

Figure 5.16. Combination Job Aid for Managing I/O Ports

Prime Computers, Inc., developed a job aid to help computer analysts to manage input/output (I/O) ports. Overall, the job aid uses the step format to guide the user through a procedure. However, Step 6 requires the user to select the next appropriate action. Figure 5.16 (above) shows a portion of this job aid, which combines steps and decision-table job aids.

Which Format is Best for a Particular Situation?

When deciding on a format for job aids, Ruth, the supervisor of training for a utility company, should begin by asking herself the following five questions:

1. Is the task or job composed of a series of steps?
2. Does the task or job require written responses and calculations?
3. Does the task or job require access to an extensive or changing body of data?
4. Does the task or job rely on decision making?
5. Is there one correct answer or action that results from the process?

Figure 5.17, a decision table, shows how these answers help in the selection of a job-aid format.

The step and work-sheet formats are used for jobs or tasks that require the performer to follow steps. The array format is used for jobs or tasks that require reference to infrequently used, large, or volatile bodies of information. The decision-table and flow-chart formats are used to facilitate decision making when there is a clear-cut answer. The checklist format is also used to facilitate decision making but is used in cases in which there is no clear-cut answer and the user must draw from training and experience in order to approach the job or task. Checklists provide the user with a short list of critical information to consider before, during, or after the performance of a task.

The next section of this chapter expands the descriptions of these formats, providing more guidelines for their appropriate use and additional examples.

When to Use the Step Format

1. *The job consists of steps that must be performed in a sequence.* The step format is used primarily when the job or task is procedural. For instance, the following job aid offers directions for opening a can of tennis balls:

a. Lift tab.
b. Peel back.

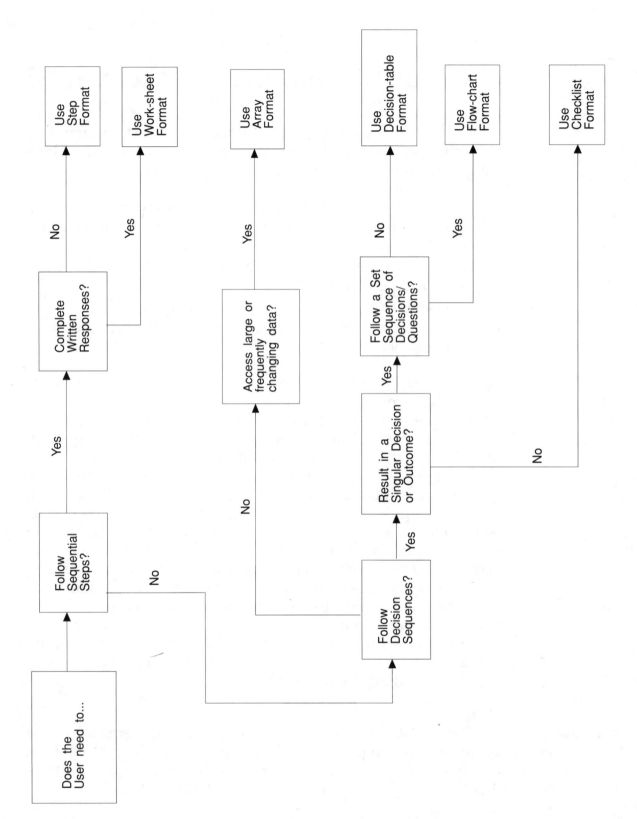

Figure 5.17. How to Select the Appropriate Format for a Job Aid

This surprising little job aid is on the metal seal of the tennis-ball can and is bolstered by a graphic representation of the procedure.

2. *The directions are simple.* Directions are simple if they can be condensed into a sentence or two. When directions are more complicated, consider using other formats.

3. *There is one path through the procedure.* The steps format does not ask the user to make binary or if-then decisions. There is no branching based on responses.

When to Use the Work-Sheet Format

1. *The job or task consists of steps that must be performed in a sequence.*

2. *The directions are simple.*

3. *There is one path through the procedure.*

4. *The user will complete written responses because of questions posed by the job aid.*

A work sheet consists of simple steps, actions, and computations to be performed by the user. For example, the work-sheet format helps a user to compute the amount of cement needed to construct a portion of a backyard patio. In this example the user first would calculate the area to be cemented and then would determine the necessary amounts of water, sand, and cement. The end product then would be little more than mixing the ingredients and pouring them into the appropriate area. In addition, such a work sheet might provide remedial help, such as guiding the user through the steps for calculating the area of a rectangle, which would then be used to calculate the area to be cemented for the patio.

When to Use the Array Format

1. *The job or task involves reference to data, not the need to execute a series of steps in order.* Array formats support information, not procedures. The user searches through a body of information for answers to questions about "who," "what," or "where." For example, the user of a dictionary needs to check either the correct spelling of a word or its meaning.

2. *The data are organized in such a way as to facilitate access to them.* The array format is based on the creation and presentation of the data in a logical and meaningful order. The order can be based on the nature of the data; for example, certain data may be arrayed in alphabetical or geographical order. Order also might be derived from the functions of the data, such as the kinds of questions they an-

swer. Contemporary technology, in fact, is particularly suited to the array format, which enables users to search through data in many ways.

3. *There is no one starting point for entry into the information and no structured path through it.* With an array format, users can find answers to "who," "what," or "where" questions.

When to Use the Decision-Table Format

1. *The user can enter at any point, depending on individual circumstances.* The decision-table job aid does not consist of steps that must be performed in a sequence. A decision-table format implies a dynamic relationship between the problem and the solution. The example of choosing a benefits brochure (Figure 5.6) shows how the characteristics of the challenge, rather than any steps or order, are critical. The user identifies the situation at hand, locates that condition in the table, and finds the correct answer or action.

2. *Several conditions or variables are associated with the job or task.* The example of choosing the benefits brochure (Figure 5.6) includes eight possible presenting conditions, each of which leads the user to a different brochure.

3. *The number of choices or options is limited.* The goal of the decision-table format is to enable the user to run a finger across a row and down a column. Once the number of possible solutions becomes excessive, the table becomes cumbersome.

When to Use the Flow-Chart Format

1. *A series of binary ("yes" or "no") decisions must be made in a particular order.*

2. *A clear path to a solution or conclusion exists.* The path to the conclusion is based on the user's selection of "yes" or "no" as answers to the questions that are posed.

3. *The movement through the process is self-explanatory.* After answering "yes" or "no" questions, the user is directed to the most appropriate answer or action. There is no need for directions.

4. *Usually more than three or four binary decisions must be made before the solution is determined.* Long mental decision sequences are cumbersome. The flow-chart format prompts the process, encouraging the user to consider all the variables before making a decision.

When to Use a Checklist Format

1. *It is a difficult, new, or ambiguous challenge that requires the user to consider many factors.* Generally checklists prompt the thought processes by which the user draws a

conclusion or makes an assessment. Checklists sometimes—but not always—provide a range of suggested approaches or answers. At other times, checklists just prompt ways of operating or of approaching a topic. Checklist job aids help the user to exercise good judgment.

2. Experience or familiarity contributes to the user's ability to profit from a checklist job aid. A novice user is least likely to profit from a checklist. This format for job aids is best used by individuals with at least a little experience with the task, who then use the checklist as a coach or adviser rather than as the initial source of performance support.

3. Order is not a key factor in the job or task. Checklists do not consist of activities performed in order. Rather, they present guidelines, attributes, points, or questions that lead the user through a mental process. Often the user is already familiar with the information and needs just a reminder.

4. The user needs guidance on how to solve a problem that has no one clear solution. A checklist provides information to help the user to determine which approach or perspective is most appropriate. Checklists usually do not identify a single answer or action.

5. Many aspects, ideas, policies, concerns, and so on must be considered. The information is usually familiar and extensive. A checklist is used before, during, and after performing the job. A shopping or packing list is an example of this characteristic of a checklist job aid.

When to Use Combined Formats

1. The situation is complex and must be supported in several ways. The Prime Computers example (Figure 5.16) uses a combination of the steps and decision-table formats. The decision-table format enables the developer to draw attention to the decision point without a lengthy explanation.

2. The directions are lengthy or difficult to understand. In such a situation, it is useful to augment the chosen formats with a step format. The basic rule of thumb is that directions should be comprehensible in a sentence or two. If they are not, then it is advisable to add a substep job aid or a separate aid that supports them.

What Means are Available to Deliver Job Aids?

Today most job aids are delivered through print or something called *extended print*. Extended print means that the job aid might be printed in many sizes on many surfaces, such as plastic, adhesive tape, cardboard, metal, laminated materials, and so on. The numbers that label the sprockets of a 35-millimeter film projector to guide the user through the process of threading it are examples of extended-print job aids.

Although print is the most typical medium for job aids, other media are gaining momentum as trainers attempt to support people in circumstances in which print is not appropriate, such as in the dark or while driving a car.

How, for example, might Jorge develop job aids for workers who are restricted from using printed or paper job aids because they work in water, work at a terminal with no desk space, or must keep their eyes on the road? Jorge has a host of choices for developing his job aid. He may choose an alternate form of print, such as laminated 3" x 5" cards that workers can keep in their pockets even while working in water. Alternatively, he might consider using on-line help screens for people working at terminals or audiotape coaching systems for those who drive as part of their jobs.

In an article in *Performance and Instruction,* Snow and Newby (1989) contend that job-aid accessibility is the key consideration, particularly when an error might produce severe consequences. Job aids such as telephone listings, charts, keys, control labels, or descriptions of emergency procedures should be readily available at the location of task performance, especially in the following situations:

- When the operator is prevented from moving (for example, an automobile driver in rush-hour traffic or an equipment operator who must constantly monitor traffic); or
- If time is a critical aspect of task performance (for example, notifying the fire department or shutting down equipment in an emergency situation).

In these situations, the need to look through a three-inch-thick telephone book or to leave the work station to access vital information can be costly and/or dangerous.

Print job aids, in the form of posters or "extended job aids," are appropriate to use when delivering step, array, decision-table, flow-chart, and checklist job aids. The familiar "Choking Victim" job aid is an example of a step aid displayed on the wall of restaurants in the United States. Another example is found on the walls of many tennis courts: "Did you remember to turn off the lights?"

These job aids are useful because they are accessible. The "Choking Victim" job aid is a familiar sight, and people know that in an emergency they will not need to look far to find one. The tennis-court sign is usually posted on all exits, so that departing players cannot miss it.

Signs or posters are not appropriate for a work-sheet job aid because the user needs a personal copy on which to make notes and computations. A work sheet must be delivered in individual copies, either through print or through computerized work stations.

Figure 5.18 matches the six job-aids formats with the appropriate media.

	Print-Poster	Extended Print	On-Line	Audio	Video
Step Format	Yes	Yes	Yes	Yes	Yes
Work-Sheet Format	No	Yes	Yes	No	No
Array Format	Yes	Yes	Yes	Yes	No
Decision-Table Format	Yes	Yes	Yes	Yes	No
Flow-Chart Format	Yes	Yes	Yes	Yes	No
Checklist Format	Yes	Yes	Yes	Yes	No

Figure 5.18. The Match Between Job-Aid Formats and Media

Audiotape job aids are becoming more common, especially in the telecommunications industry. Such job aids guide users through a series of questions, like those used in arrays, decision tables, or flow charts. The electronic voice that answers and sometimes initiates business calls is a common example. The caller responds to a question by pushing buttons on a touch-tone telephone, and the system presents another question or provides an answer keyed to the individual circumstance. These systems enhance an organization's ability to provide personalized service at reduced cost.

Videotape job aids are especially appropriate for use with the step format. The video component can simplify technical jargon and can demonstrate techniques, such as the way to hold a tennis racket in order to execute a perfect serve. Video gives the user the power to stop, review, and practice procedures and provides a video model to compare with individual performance as a form of feedback.

Computers are growing in popularity based on their abilities to do many things; delivering job aids is just one of them. In her book, *Making CBT Happen,* Gloria Gery defines on-line (computer-delivered) job aids as "...resources...that are immediately and easily accessible to a software user actively engaged in the software itself" (1987, p. 207). On-line job aids are often accessed through menus that help the user through a process or procedure; such job aids can check spelling, identify the meaning of an error message, or list the steps to print a document. A checklist and work-sheet job aid that an insurance agent uses to present information to a client could also be delivered as an on-line job aid. The computer program might help the agent to complete a pre-qualification determination, using a checklist to ensure basic eligibility. The software then would guide the agent through a work sheet to compute the premium. Chapter 11 provides detailed coverage of technology and job aids, with a focus on on-line help, expert, and performance-support systems.

Review of Chapter 5

What is a format?

- A job aid format is the way information is presented to the user.

What choices exist?

- Steps;
- Work sheet;
- Array;
- Decision table;
- Flow chart;
- Checklist; or
- Combination.

How does one choose which format to use? Choosing a format depends on the primary job or task to be performed, based on the following considerations:

- Is the task or job composed of a series of steps?

- Does the task or job require written responses and calculations?
- Does the task or job require access to an extensive or changing body of data?
- Does the task or job rely on decision making?
- Is there one correct answer or action that results from the process?

What are the means for delivering job aids?

- Paper (poster and extended);
- On-line computer display;
- Audiotape; and
- Videotape.

Preview of Chapter 6

Chapter 5 presented the six job-aid formats and matched those formats with appropriate media. Chapter 6 lists general rules to follow when developing job aids and specific rules to follow when developing steps, work-sheet, decision-table, flow-chart, or checklist job aids. It also includes methods for ensuring that the job aid works.

References

Buzinski, A. (1987). Worksheet for pricing training proposals. *Performance and Instruction, 26*(6), 26.

Clark, R. (1986). Defining the "D" in ISD: Part 2: Task-specific instructional methods. *Performance and Instruction, 25*(3), 12-17.

Geis, G. (1984). Checklisting. *Journal of Instructional Development, 7*(1), 2-9.

Gery, G. (1987). *Making CBT happen.* Boston, MA: Weingarten Publications.

Harless, J.H. (1988). *Job aids workshop.* Paper presented at Job Aids Workshop by Harless Guild and Associates, Atlanta, GA.

Rossett, A. (1987). *Training needs assessment.* Englewood Cliffs, NJ: Educational Technology Publications.

Snow, N., & Newby, T. (1989). Ergonomically Designed Job Aids. *Performance and Instruction, 28*(3), 26-30.

Steps for Developing Job Aids

Bill, a training-support manager for a department store chain, is beginning to work on an emergency-exit job aid. During an emergency, all employees are responsible for assisting customers to appropriate exits. What steps should he follow to develop such a job aid? Are there any rules?

Susan, a human-resources specialist for a pharmaceutical company, is asked to introduce a new expense-reporting procedure. How can she help off-site sales personnel to learn how to complete their new expense claims?

How can Karen make sure that a job aid is effective before her organization invests in production, duplication, and distribution? How can Karen increase the chances that employees will use the job aid?

Chapter 6 provides guidance for these people and other professionals by answering one key question: What are the steps to follow for developing a job aid?

The job-aid development process involves the following six steps:

1. Clarify the problem to be solved by the job aid.
2. Choose the format and medium.

3. Prepare a draft of the job aid.
4. Pilot the job aid.
5. Make revisions to the job aid.
6. Manage the job aid.

These steps assume that a job aid has already been determined to be the appropriate solution to the problem (see Chapter 3). The following are descriptions and illustrations of these six steps.

Step 1: Clarify the Problem to Be Solved by the Job Aid

As is the case with any training, the first step in developing a job aid is to identify and focus on the problem to be solved. *Training Needs Assessment* (Rossett, 1987) is a good source of detailed information on needs assessment. Step 1 takes into consideration how to collect information and how to use the characteristics of the job itself to plan the job aid.

Three types of information commonly would be collected during a needs assessment:

1. The best way of doing or approaching the task;
2. The common errors or misjudgments made by users; and
3. The kind and level of help needed by the user.

How to Collect Information

Information can be collected in the following three ways: through observations, through interviews, and through performance of the job or task by the developer of the job aid. When possible, all three methods of collecting information should be used. The emphasis and time spent on each type of data-collection technique will depend on the job, task, or mental process involved. Observations should be emphasized when the job or task is observable; interviews should be emphasized when the job or task relies on mental processes such as decision making. Another useful technique is for the developer to actually try doing the job.

Once the plan for gathering information has been developed, the observer or interviewer contacts the manager or supervisor of the people who will be observed or interviewed. This is important to ensure access to the performers.

Observations. Job observations usually include two phases. First, the job-aid developer reviews the information that supports the job or task. This information might include documentation, policy and procedure manuals, training manuals, and information about errors or customer complaints. This observation is often completed during the initial needs-assessment stage. The information found in these documents focuses observations at the job site.

The second phase of observation happens at the job site. There the developer can see how the job is performed in the work environment by expert, typical, and novice performers. At this stage, the developer takes explicit notes and records deviations from how the model or expert approaches the job.

Interviews. The interview provides an opportunity for the developer to build from observations and to delve more deeply into differences or similarities in performance and outcome. The interview is the developer's primary tool for collecting information about the process, for finding out what the performer is thinking and feeling, and for shedding light on decision making. Interviews, unlike observations, provide flexibility because there are opportunities for the interviewer to ask for clarification. Interviews also create a personal connection between the developer and the performer that might encourage use of the job aid once it has been completed.

Interviews answer the following questions:

- What is the performer thinking about while performing the job or task?

- What kinds of information and details do performers need?

- Why did the performer do it that way? Why are others approaching it differently?

- Might special circumstances arise to change the way the job or task is performed or approached?

- Are there steps or stages that are particularly difficult or often forgotten?

- How would the performer feel about using a job aid?

For a job or task that cannot be observed directly, a two-phase interview is useful. First, the performer talks spontaneously; the developer asks general and open-ended questions to get an overview of the process and to determine differences between the performances of experts and novices. Some companies assemble juries of experts for this stage of the process. These juries, Rossett (1987, p. 176) notes, "quickly gather information, dispense information, and build affiliation."

The second stage seeks more specific information and employs more directed questions. For example, during the first phase of interviews with people who write for non-English speakers, the interviewer might have learned "When finished writing a document for non-English speakers, I always review the document to ensure the use of simple sentences." The developer might follow up in the second interview with questions such as "What do you consider to be a simple sentence? How many words does it have? How long are the words? Any exceptions?" The answers to both phases of questions have obvious implications for the job aid.

Personal performance of the job. Performance of the job by the developer provides a deeper understanding of what has been seen and heard. The developer can use personal trials to identify tricky or confusing steps or processes. Personal performance of the job is especially useful in developing job aids for novice users. In many ways, the developer is like the novice. Personal performance shows where novices have problems. Of course, in many cases, personal trials are impossible because the job is dangerous or because it requires special skills. In these cases, the developer relies more heavily on observations and interviews.

How to Use the Characteristics of the Job to Create the Job Aid

Subject-matter or task analysis basically involves collecting enough information to break the job, task, or mental process into very small steps or organized chunks of information. This process enables the developer to identify the true characteristics of the performance.

Data collection for job-aid development should follow the natural and usually chronological progression of the job or task. The developer watches the process or procedure from start to finish just as the job is performed in the work environment, always pressing the performer about what he or she does or is thinking about in order to perform the job. This process turns debates over philosophies and theories into data about what to do, what to consider, and how to accomplish the task.

Before: What does the performer need to know, do, or have before he or she can do the job or task? At this point, the developer identifies the prerequisites for doing the job. Because job aids are about performance, the best place to start is to watch a worker prepare to do the job. Is everything established prior to the performance? Is location important? For example, does the user need to do the job on a flat surface or in a cool or quiet place? The developer identifies similarities and differences in how novices and experts prepare. He or she lists or describes the preparation process and notes the names of tools and possibly brief descriptions or drawings of tools. Should the preparation stage be included as part of the job aid, or should it be supported by an additional job aid, by training, or by a presentation from a supervisor?

During: What is typically done? Are there ever special circumstances or special safety considerations? The developer determines how the person actually performs the job or task. What are the major steps or skills needed to perform it? How is it usually accomplished? The developer asks the performer to do what he or she would usually do if no one were observing. The developer notes every observable action in detail. During the observation or just after it, the developer asks the performer about what he or she is thinking. How does the performer approach the problem? How does he or she proceed to solve the problem? What does he or she do or think about and in what order? Does every performer follow the same order? Does it matter? Are there times when the performer must follow different steps? Might a condition arise to warrant developing a supporting job aid, such as a job aid for "saving information to a disk"? What if the inserted disk is full? How is that handled? How is another disk inserted? What if the user lacks another formatted disk?

After: What does the performer need to do on completion of the job or task? What does the performer do once the widget is assembled or the program is debugged or the performance appraisal is completed? Does the performer run the program one last time, then save it to disk and scribble his or her initials on the label? Are there any special precautions or reminders? For example, a job aid that supports the assembly of an electrical device may end with the following note: "IMPORTANT: RECHECK THAT ALL SOLDERED CONNECTIONS ARE TAPED WITH BLACK ELECTRICAL TAPE." These end notes or final steps are especially useful for novice users who may not understand the entire process (the need to scribble initials on the disk) or who may be more likely to fumble a particular step and therefore need to recheck more carefully.

Step 2: Choose the Format and Medium

The job or task is the key to choosing a format; Chapter 5 offers descriptions for choosing a format and medium. Other important considerations include the following: Who will be using the job aid? What is the working environment? What resources are available?

Who Will Be Using the Job Aid?

How much experience do the users have? Job aids developed for novice performers or frequently changing users often require more detail. The 1040 form (Figure 5.14) was developed for novice users. The primary format is a work sheet, but because it was developed for novice or infrequent users, it includes a comprehensive step job aid.

What is the user's ability to read or understand English? Statistics show that nearly 25 percent of all English-speaking adults are functionally illiterate. Therefore, it may be beneficial to augment the job aid with graphics, audiotapes, or videotapes.

What kind of documentation is familiar to the user? When documentation is commonplace for a job, use a familiar format. For example, computer programmers often use flow charts to depict the development of a program. Therefore, given the choice of a decision-table or a flow-chart job aid, the developer would choose a flow chart. A job aid should blend into the work environment; the user should not be forced to struggle with an unfamiliar format.

Does the user want to perform? Chapter 3 addresses this issue, but it is so important and relevant to the development of job aids that it deserves a second mention. A job aid is not an appropriate tool for erasing employee resistance, because the employee probably will not choose to use it.

What Is the Working Environment?

Where will the job aid be used? The appropriate job aid would differ depending on whether it was to be used while the user's hands were tied up fixing a sink, while working in the dark, or while at a computer terminal. Information about the environment in which the job aid will be used helps to determine the best medium to use. The developer considers the conditions of the environment, then determines how best to present the job aid so it fits into the environment.

What Job-Aid Development Resources Are Available?

Who is available to work on the job aid? When planning a job aid, the developer needs to ensure that the right people will be available. Job-aid development might require a team consisting of the following:

- Instructional designers, training specialists, or human resource development professionals;
- Graphic artists;

■ Subject-matter experts; and

■ Computer programmers for on-line job aids.

How much time is available? Sometimes job aids are needed to solve immediate problems, such as Susan's need to help her managers complete the new expense-claim report. She may choose to develop a "quick-and-dirty job aid." This kind of job aid solves the problem at hand and is often redeveloped when time allows.

How much money has been allocated? Job aids are less expensive than training. Joe Harless (1988) suggests that job aids are three to four times less expensive than training. He notes that the real savings happen because workers remain at the site and are productive, whereas for training they would be absent and nonproductive. Consider the amount of time it takes to develop a twenty-page print-based training package. Contrast this with how long it takes to deliver that training. How many people attend the training session? How much do they earn? How much does it cost for them to travel to the training and for their room and board? When these costs are combined, the impact of job aids on the bottom line is striking.

Choose the Format

The work completed thus far should provide a clear picture of the job or task. The following steps are used to determine the format:

1. Decide what part of the task or job is being supported by the job aid.
2. Consider the data about the user's background, level of experience, and previous experience with documentation.
3. Use Figure 5.17 to determine which format or combination of formats is best.

Choose the Medium

Cost is a factor in choosing a medium. For example, an on-line job aid is much more expensive than a printed one. The medium is determined after considering the format, working environment, and budgetary constraints. Automation would be warranted only if the number of users were large and the content were stable. Chapter 5 provides an explanation of the considerations and implications of using one medium over another, and Figure 5.18 serves as a guide for choosing a medium.

Step 3: Prepare a Draft of the Job Aid

The development team needs to be called together. When the team consists only of a designer and a subject-matter expert, this time is used to organize information. If the team is larger, the initial session is used to explain the process of drafting a job aid, including how the format and medium were chosen and the role that each person will play. It may also be useful to describe budget and time constraints.

The information collected in Step 1 is used to break each major task into smaller, subordinate steps or skills. For example, Figure 6.1 illustrates the steps for completing a tune-up. One step in this process is to replace the spark plugs. By observing a mechanic performing an automobile tune-up, the developer witnessed the procedure for removing spark plugs. Through interviews, the developer learned that one of the subordinate steps for replacing spark plugs is to choose the appropriate replacement spark plug. The interviewer also learned that the novice performer might be unsure about which spark plug to use, because the code numbers are different from brand to brand. Therefore, for the step "Replace spark plugs," the developer must include a decision-table job aid to ensure that the novice chooses the correct spark plug every time. This also might require meeting with a subject-matter expert to determine considerations for the decision table. By breaking the job into small steps and substeps, the developer provides prompts when the user needs them.

The developer of a job aid usually begins by listing the steps or information the user needs in order to complete the task. If order is important, the developer puts the steps in the correct order. Then, if the process is a decision sequence, the developer lists all possible conditions and the appropriate responses. After listing all the routine steps, the developer identifies places or times when special circumstances might arise, making an effort to account for every possible situation that the user might encounter while doing the job or task.

Susan Zagorski (1987) suggests listing the steps or information that the user needs immediately after he or she has completed the job or task. For example, a final note on a job aid designed to help people to prepare bulk-mail packages might read, "You are now ready to bring your mail to the 'Bulk Mail' Department of the Central Post Office." This step is not really a part of the preparation of bulk-mail packages, but it is a crucial part of the overall process. Other needed

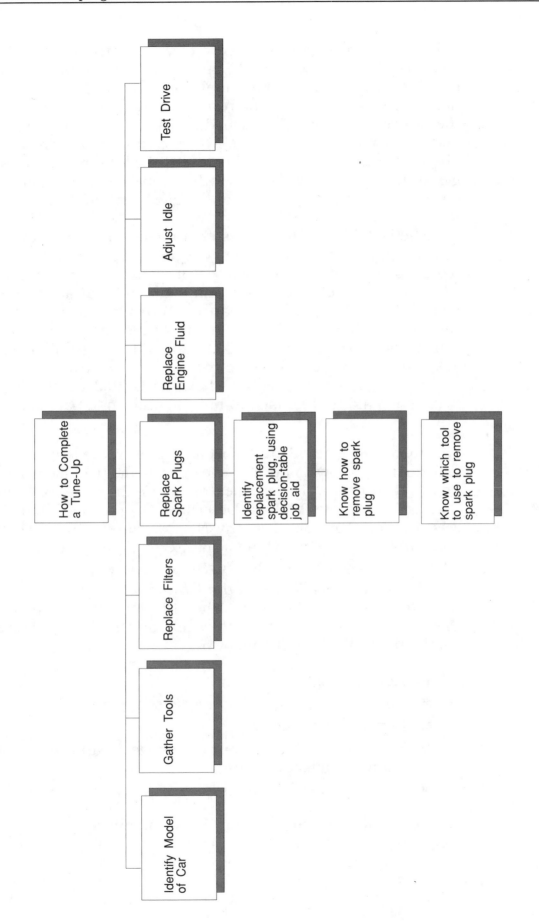

Figure 6.1. Combination Job Aid for Completing an Automobile Tune-Up

information may be drawn from common errors. For example, every step of the United States Federal Income Tax work sheet is supported by a thorough explanation; however, a final job aid is printed on the return envelope that reads "Sign the return? Organize your schedules and forms in proper order? Use your pre-printed label? Keep a copy for your records?" These crucial last steps are often overlooked. Sometimes a single statement will suffice. At other times, a developer may choose a supplemental job aid, based on what he or she knows about the user.

The last part of the process is to develop a rough draft of the primary job aid, using the chosen format. Then draft and redraft statements to eliminate extra words, to combine ideas that belong together, and to eliminate ideas that are ambiguous. This draft is crucial because it provides the infrastructure for the job aid. The statements must be as clean and lean as possible. Before giving the job aid to a graphic artist, ask a subject-matter expert to review it for accuracy.

For example, Figure 6.2 shows a United States Postal Service job aid that is used to bundle bulk-mail packages.

General Rules for Job-Aid Development

The following general and specific rules represent experts' agreement on how to develop clear and effective documentation and job aids. These rules draw on the work of Phyllis Balan, Zane Berge, William Deterline, George Geis, Joe Harless, Patricia Lawson, Timothy Newby, Nancy Snow, Harold Stolovitch, Sivasailam Thiagarajan, Sylvie Vanasse, Stephen Yelon, Susan Zagorski, and others.

Concentrate on "how" in the job aid's title or on what exactly the aid does for users. The title tells the users what they will be able to do when they rely on the job aid. For example, they will know the following:

- How to program a VCR;
- Considerations in selecting a used car;
- How to cook an owl;
- How to make sure your language is appropriate for limited-English readers;
- Ways to approach an employee grievance hearing.

Construct statements that are clear and direct. Use direct, pithy language and avoid long or unfamiliar words. For example, the following statements are clear and direct:

- Turn the screw 360° ; and

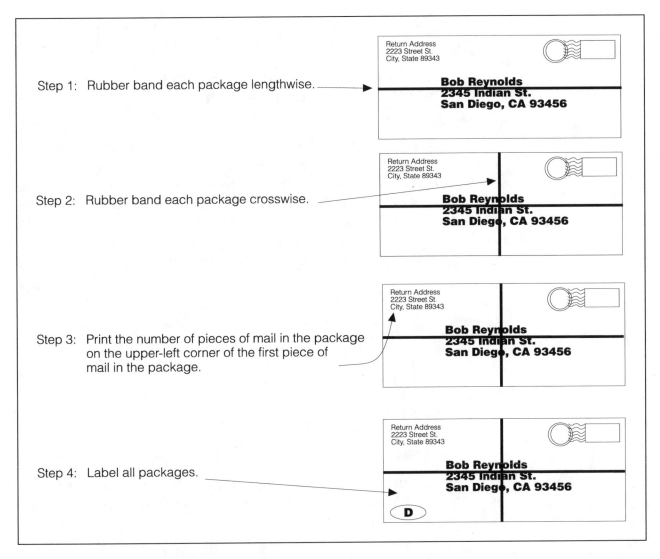

Figure 6.2. Step Job Aid for Preparing Bulk-Mail Packages

- READ the safety instructions BEFORE beginning work.

Use the user's vocabulary. For example, it is appropriate to use jargon when it is the language used by all job-aid users. For example, if the users are structural engineers, it would be appropriate to direct them to "Set the polysides to 2."

Provide examples when appropriate. Examples provide additional support. This is especially important for job aids that are developed for both novices and experts. The example may be important for the novice, but the expert will use the main support information and skip over the examples.

Lead with action verbs and highlight those verbs. When possible, put the action word first. Highlight the action by putting the verb in uppercase letters or boldface type. For example, the following are examples of good job-aid steps:

- PUSH the button firmly until it snaps into place;
- TWIST the knob until it is tight; or
- ASK the new employee for two forms of identification.

Emphasize action but do not ignore "why." When no introduction to the job aid is planned, some employees may doubt the importance of the information. In these cases it will be useful to provide brief explanations of what the employee is asked to do and why. Figure 6.3 gives an example of a job aid that addresses the "what" and the "why."

Present information in small bits. The user should be able to glance at the information and to have that glance influence performance. Harless (1988) suggests writing short sentences and using short words to describe or list the following:

- A single step;
- A single calculation;
- A single decision sequence;
- A single idea; or
- A list of related attributes.

Use graphics and drawings. Pictures speak a thousand words. They describe details as well as actions without long-winded explanations. Pictures serve the following functions:

- Accentuating important information;
- Clarifying ideas and points;

```
┌─────────────────────────────────────────┐
│               Checklist                  │
│                                          │
│      Action                   Why*       │
│                                          │
│  1. _____         C   R  (S)  Sp   │
│                                          │
│  2. _____         C  (R)  S  (Sp)  │
│                                          │
│  3. _____        (C)  R   S   Sp   │
│                                          │
│  4. _____         C  (R)  S   Sp   │
│                                          │
│  *C=Cost  R=Customer Response  S=Safety  Sp=Speed │
└─────────────────────────────────────────┘
```

**Figure 6.3. Checklist Job Aid That
Addresses "What" and "Why"**

- Showing more detail than words can show; and
- Putting the job or task into the user's perspective.

In her article, "The Job Aid as Zen Art," Susan Zagorski (1989) illustrates this point through the example shown in Figure 6.4. The text box describes the process of opening a jar of miso; the figure box shows graphically how it is done.

Following are suggestions for using graphics effectively:

- Draw attention to a crucial idea or actions by using boldface type, boxes, italics, uppercase letters, underlining, and solid arrows.

- Use line drawings to support words. Keep drawings simple; include only essential details. *Avoid* photographs, because they show too much detail (Harless, 1988).

- Weigh the costs and benefits of using color over black-and-white drawings. Color reproduction is very expensive, but "research indicates visual search times can be reduced by 50-70% by using color codes" (Snow & Newby, 1989, p. 28).

- Use three-quarter-size drawings when possible. The human eye converts these drawings to full size (Harless, 1988).

- Place illustrations on the left side of the page.

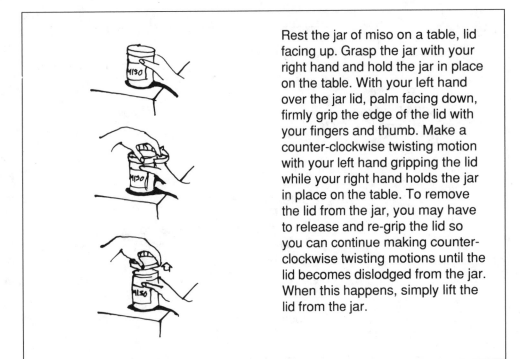

Rest the jar of miso on a table, lid facing up. Grasp the jar with your right hand and hold the jar in place on the table. With your left hand over the jar lid, palm facing down, firmly grip the edge of the lid with your fingers and thumb. Make a counter-clockwise twisting motion with your left hand gripping the lid while your right hand holds the jar in place on the table. To remove the lid from the jar, you may have to release and re-grip the lid so you can continue making counter-clockwise twisting motions until the lid becomes dislodged from the jar. When this happens, simply lift the lid from the jar.

Figure 6.4. How to Open a Jar of Miso

- Let the illustration speak for itself. Add words to prompt or to describe the process further. For example, Figure 6.5 shows a job aid with a minimum of written explanation.

- Use white space or lines to separate information and steps. Job aids should not look cluttered. The user should be able to scan the page quickly while doing a job or task. The organization of the information should be clear at first glance.

- Ensure that the job aid is accessible. This is especially important when the user cannot move away from the job or when the consequences of error are severe. Most users will not search through a file cabinet or on others' desks to find a job aid. An inaccessible job aid is one that will not be used.

Specific Rules for Job Aid Development

Step Job Aids

- The step format is used for jobs that require the user to follow steps in sequence. Make that sequence clear.
- Number or letter the steps.
- Make certain that each step represents only one process or procedure.

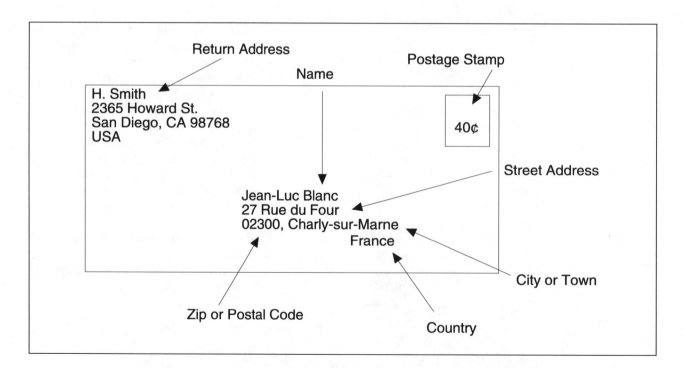

Figure 6.5. How to Address an Overseas Envelope

Work-Sheet Job Aids

- The work-sheet format also requires the user to follow steps in sequence. Again, make that sequence clear.
- Number or letter each step of the calculation.
- Ask the question before providing space for the response. For example:

  STEP 1. What size is the AREA to be cemented?
  AREA = Length x Width = _____ sq. ft.

- Make work sheets free-standing. The work sheet should be completely separate, or the user should be able to separate the form easily from the documentation that supports it. It is cumbersome to require the user to turn back and forth between instructions and the work sheet.

Array Job Aids

- The array format is used for jobs that require the user to refer to bodies of information. Organize the data in a format with obvious meaning, either based on their nature or on the structure of demands that users will place on the data.
- Organize the data logically.
- Because the array format is often used for data that change frequently, the user needs to know the specific version of data that the job aid fits. For example, computer software companies distribute mats that fit over computer keyboards and correspond to function keys. In order for the job aid to be effective, the user needs to know to what version of software the mat accompanies.

Decision-Table Job Aids

- Work backward when developing decision tables. Decide where the user will finish and then identify the factors that will lead the user there.
- List all possible solutions or responses to *if* statements. The responses are the *then* statements. They define all the possible solutions.
- Determine the conditions or chain of factors that lead to solutions or responses.

■ Determine the number of columns needed by adding the categories of possible conditions and responses or by adding the if, and, and then statements.

For example, in Figure 6.6, the conditions from which the personnel clerk will determine which benefits brochure to provide are the following:

■ If the Department is...
■ And the Employee is hourly,
■ Then provide brochure number....

In this case, the table must contain three columns.

Department	Hourly Employee	Benefits Brochure No.
Maintenance	Yes	123
	No	50
Housekeeping	Yes	136
	No	52
Food Service	Yes	148
	No	53
Sales	Yes	152
	No	54

**Figure 6.6. Decision-Table Job Aid for
Choosing a Benefits Brochure**

■ List the conditions in the order that they will probably present themselves to the employee on the job. In the preceding example, the personnel clerk gets clues about the employee's department from his or her uniform. Because it is the employee's uniform that the personnel clerk sees first, this condition is presented first. The personnel clerk must then ask the employee whether he or she is hourly or salaried. Therefore, this condition is presented second.

■ A decision table leads the user to one answer. Be sure that each decision sequence leads to only one possible answer. For decision sequences with more than one possible answer, use a checklist format.

■ Column headers are best written as open-ended statements or questions, such as in the following examples:

If the form is_____, then send to _____.
When the light flashes _____ then call _____.

Flow Charts

- The process for drafting a flow chart is similar to the process for drafting a decision table. List all possible solutions or responses; these are the statements that define the end of the sequence. For example, Figure 6.7 leads the user to one of two possible solutions: "Use an Outside Contractor" or "Use In-House Staff."

- Develop a series of binary (true/false or yes/no) questions that lead to each of the possible solutions or responses. In Figure 6.7, the following questions were used: Is in-house staff available for assignment? Does

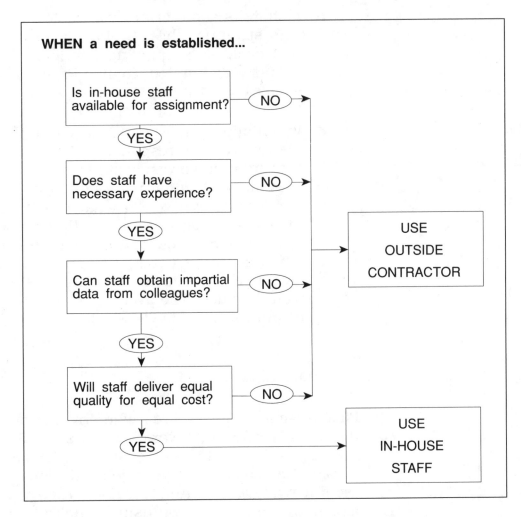

Figure 6.7. Flow-Chart Job Aid for Selecting Contractors

staff have necessary experience? Can staff obtain impartial data from colleagues? Will staff deliver equal quality for equal cost?

■ Draw a diagram that represents the progression of statements leading to the end response. The flow chart will look more ordered when the lines are horizontal and vertical, not diagonal (Harless, 1988). Avoid crossed lines because they are confusing to the user.

Checklists

■ List the conditions or structure questions in the order in which the user is to consider them.

■ Provide enough information to help guide the user to the appropriate solution.

■ If there is some clear progression of information, use it to structure the job aid. For example, Figure 5.12, "A Checklist Simplifying Language When Writing for People with Limited English Proficiency" begins with a simple consideration (length of words) and works its way to determining the presence of complex verb phrases.

■ When appropriate, list or describe the range of possible answers or responses. Checklists do not always lead to a single response, but may lead to a range of responses. If this range is defined, include it. For example, a new book on what to eat during pregnancy provides categories of foods that must be represented in a woman's diet. These categories include proteins, foods containing vitamin C, calcium-rich foods, and so on. If a dietician were using this book, this list would suffice. The average user, however, would need examples of the foods within these categories.

Step 4: Pilot the Job Aid

Pilot testing is the process whereby the developer tries out the job aid with "real-world" end users. Steve Stum (1987) puts the utility of this step best when he says, "Let's face the music and dance. Test your job aid; you face the music to see if it really works. And if it does, then you can dance!" (p. 22). If the job aid is confusing, unclear, or inaccessible, it will not be used.

The first step in pilot testing is to choose a test group that is representative of end users. Make sure the group represents the full range of performers. Implement the job aid just as if it were being released in final form. For example, if the job aid will be taped to an instrument panel or chained to the side of a conveyor belt, then the job aid should be pilot tested there. Ask employees to use the job aid to perform the task. Observe their performance and then interview them about the performance and outcomes.

The following checklist helps the developer to identify any problems with the job aid:

Pilot Testing Job Aids

Ask the user:

1. *Do you have any questions?*
2. *Were you unsure at any time?*
3. *Were there steps that were harder to follow than others?*
4. *Was the job aid difficult to use at your work station?*
5. *Were the instructions clear?*
6. *Were the steps ordered correctly?*
7. *Were there times when you needed more information?*
8. *Were there times when there was too much information?*
9. *Was the wording of the job aid clear?*
10. *Were the diagrams or graphs helpful?*
11. *Were there typographical errors?*
12. *Did a circumstance arise that was not covered in the job aid?*
13. *Should any special circumstances be covered in the job aid?*
14. *Will you use it again?*
15. *Do you wish that you and your colleagues had a copy of this job aid?*

Step 5: Make Revisions to the Job Aid

Use the information collected in Step 4 to develop the final version of the job aid. Once all revisions have been implemented, obtain the final sign-off from subject-matter experts and management and develop the master copy of the job aid. The job aid then can be reproduced and packaged for the kind of distribution that has been carefully selected to support it.

Step 6: Manage the Job Aid

To be successful, a job aid must be managed and carefully integrated into the work environment. The first task in managing a job aid is to develop strategies to increase the chances that the job aid will be used, both initially and over time.

The fast-changing environments that make job aids desirable also threaten their usefulness over time. Job aids swiftly lose credibility if they fail to keep up with the challenges and tools they must support. Job-aid management must institutionalize ways for a job aid to change as people and their work environments change.

People. As the work force changes, does the job aid continue to meet the new work-force needs? Are the orientation, training, and coaching systems in place to help new employees use the job aid successfully?

Work Environment. Who is responsible for introducing the initial job aid? When a new product or procedure is adopted, are revisions to job aids automatic and mandatory? How will the organization keep track of all the job aids already out there? Is there a budget for revisions? These issues suggest the need for a systematic approach to managing job aids and their revisions.

The Job Aid. A job aid should clearly indicate the date of its latest revision. Snow and Newby (1989) stress the importance of making the job aid accessible to all employees when they need it. Supply more than enough job aids for every employee or work station. If a user must rely on many job aids, make sure that each job aid is discernible from the others.

A Revision System. A systematic approach to managing revisions should address the following issues:

- ■ Initiation. Who is responsible for initiating revisions? Are revisions initiated through periodic reviews, linked to changes in procedure and/or technology? Can managers easily request revisions?

- Implementation. Who implements revisions? Who collects outdated versions and introduces new versions?
- Administration. Who keeps track of the existing job aids? Can the organization list the units and positions using a particular job aid? Does everyone understand the authority and responsibility structure surrounding job aids? Is there a budget for revising job aids?
- Incentives. Who receives recognition when job aids are successful? Who is acknowledged for their proper introduction, maintenance, and revision?

Review of Chapter 6

What are the steps for developing job aids?

- **Step 1:** Clarify the problem to be solved by the job aid. How is the job performed? What kind of mental or physical process is the job aid supporting? What role will the job aid play?
- **Step 2:** Choose the format and medium. When choosing a format and medium, consider who will be using the job aid, what the working environment is like, and what resources are available.
- **Step 3:** Prepare a draft of the job aid. First, organize the information collected in Steps 1 and 2. Draft and redraft the job aid, and then follow the general rules for job-aid development.
- **Step 4:** Pilot the job aid. Use "real-world" end users and ask them to complete the job or task using the job aid. Use the "Checklist for Pilot Testing Job Aids" to identify revisions needed.
- **Step 5:** Make revisions to the job aid. Complete the revisions, get a final sign-off from subject-matter experts and management, and develop a master copy. Reproduce the job aid.
- **Step 6:** Manage the job aid. To increase the chances that the job aid will be used, ensure that the job aid is relevant and accessible. Supply more than enough job aids for every employee and work station. Develop a system that signifies that a job aid has been revised. Determine how and when revisions will be initiated, and who will initiate the revisions and remove outdated versions.

Preview of Chapters 7, 8, and 9

Chapter 7, 8, and 9 provide examples of "real-world" job aids. The chapters are divided by the way in which the job aids are used: Chapter 7 examines job aids for informing; Chapter 8 examines job aids for proceeding; and Chapter 9 examines job aids for decision making and coaching. These chapters provide useful examples from which practitioners can develop job aids to fit individual needs.

References

Balan, P. (1989). Improving instructional print materials through text design. *Performance and Instruction, 28*(7), 13-17.

Deterline, W. (1989). Some roles and rules. *Performance and Instruction, 28*(7),45-48.

Geis, G. (1984). Checklisting. *Journal of Instructional Development, 7*(1), 2-9.

Harless, J.H. (1988). *Job Aids Workshop.* Paper presented at Job Aids Workshop by Harless Guild and Associates, Atlanta, GA.

Lawson, P. (1986). Job aids: Give the readers what they want. (Report No. CE 044 648). Viewpoints. (ERIC Document Reproduction Service No. ED 273 746)

Nelson, J. (1989). Quick and dirty job aids. *Performance and Instruction, 28*(8), 35.

Rossett, A. (1987). *Training needs assessment.* Englewood Cliffs, NJ: Educational Technology Publications.

Snow, N., & Newby, T. (1989). Ergonomically designed job aids. *Performance and Instruction, 28*(3), 26-30.

Stolovitch, H., & Vanasse, S. (1989). The paradox of user documentation: Useful, but rarely used. *Performance and Instruction, 28*(7), 19-22.

Stum, S. (1987). Countdown of the top ten hits for job aid construction. *Performance and Instruction, 26*(4), 22.

Yelon, S., & Berge, Z. (1987). Using fancy checklists for efficient feedback. *Performance and Instruction, 26*(4), 14-20.

Zagorski, S. (1987). How I created the award-winning job aid. *Performance and Instruction, 26*(4), 29-32.

Zagorski, S. (1989). The job aid as Zen art. *Performance and Instruction, 28*(10), 15-20.

Zemke, R., & Kramlinger, T. (1982). *Figuring things out: A trainer's guide to needs analysis.* Boston, MA: Addison-Wesley.

Part Three

Examples of Job Aids

Job Aids for Informing

Chapter 7 offers examples of how job aids provide information. In addition, extensive interviews with the people who created and used these job aids resulted in commentaries on what worked, how it worked, and what the creators would do differently now. Their commentaries have been included within each example.

Defining Job Aids That Provide Information

Information job aids make data useful; they help the user answer questions about who, what, which, or where. Such job aids are most useful when they are organized by the user's frame of reference and when they emphasize relationships and connections. As with all other types of job aids, the information job aid must be accessible when needed: before, during, or after performance.

Examples of Job Aids for Informing

The following pages provide four examples of job aids that address typical needs for information.

Example 1

Outgoing Federal Returns and Exception Items
Quick Reference Guide:
Sovran Bank, N.A.

Need:

Sovran Bank developed this job aid in response to the Federal Reserve's new regulations that required Automated Clearing House (ACH) departments nationwide to automate and to standardize their processing and coding systems. As a result of this mandate, Sovran Bank needed to hire two new employees and train them quickly. The ACH department supervisor, working with Denise Brown in the Commercial Services Development department, determined that both the existing employee and the new employees were in need of information.

Development:

This is an example of how one financial institution successfully developed a job aid to provide quick reference to new codes and terminology. Brown reports that she and one subject-matter expert collaborated on the development of this job aid and that it cost only one hundred dollars.

The illustration in Figure 7.1 is a portion of the five-page job aid. It provides information about terminology and uses a reference-table (array) format. It is printed on 5" x 8" paper and is spiral bound. The front and back covers are card stock. Brown describes the rationale for using this size of job aid: "It's cute and therefore appealing to the ACH employees."

Delivery and Maintenance:

Two new employees used the job aid during their new-employee training. The experienced employee was given the job aid after minimal direction.

GLOSSARY

DEBIT -	A WITHDRAWAL, A TRANSACTION THAT AFFECTS THE ACCOUNT BALANCE IN A NEGATIVE DIRECTION.
DELETE -	A FUNCTION AVAILABLE FOR OUTGOING RETURNS. THE DELETE FUNCTION ALLOWS TRANSACTIONS THAT HAVE BEEN KEYED INCORRECTLY TO BE REMOVED FROM THE DATA BASE.
DESCRIPTIVE DATA -	A FIELD ON THE RETURN ENTRY SCREENS. THE PURPOSE OF THE FIELD IS FOR THE ORIGINATING DFI TO BE ABLE TO INCLUDE SPECIAL HANDLING CODES AND INFORMATION OF SIGNIFICANCE TO THEMSELVES.
DFI -	DEPOSITORY FINANCIAL INSTITUTION; A BANK, SAVINGS AND LOAN, OR CREDIT UNION.
DISCRETIONARY DATA -	A FIELD ON THE RETURN ENTRY SCREENS. THE PURPOSE OF THE FIELD IS FOR THE ORIGINATING DFI TO BE ABLE TO INCLUDE SPECIAL HANDLING CODES AND INFORMATION OF SIGNIFICANCE TO THEMSELVES.
EDC -	ELECTRONIC DELIVERY CENTRAL; RICHMOND ACH
ENTRY -	A REQUEST FOR THE DEPOSIT OF MONEY TO THE ACCOUNT OF THE RECEIVER, OR FOR THE PAYMENT OF MONEY FROM THE ACCOUNT OF THE RECEIVER.
ITEM -	A SINGLE TRANSACTION.
MTE -	MACHINE TRANSFER ENTRIES. USED TO POST AUTOMATIC TELLER MACHINE (ATM) TRANSACTIONS.
NOTIFICATION OF	AN OPTION AVAILABLE ON OUTGOING RETURNS. THE NOTIFICATION OF CHANGE OPTION ALLOWS ACH TO NOTIFY AN ORIGINATOR THAT A TRANSACTION WAS INCORRECT AND SUPPLY THE ORIGINATOR WITH THE CORRECT INFORMATION.
ON-US ENTRY -	A TRANSACTION THAT ORIGINATED AT SOVRAN AND AFFECTED ANOTHER SOVRAN ACCOUNT.
ORIGINATOR -	THE PERSON OR CORPORATION THAT CREATES THE ENTRY.

Figure 7.1. Array Job Aid for Glossary of Terms

The department uses a system whereby all job aids are scheduled for review and update every six months. When the job aids are used by a small group of workers, training personnel distribute the job aids by hand and point out changes. When the target population is large or the changes extensive, the manager of the unit affected distributes the job aids and discusses any changes.

Impact:

This job aid achieved the desired results. The Federal Reserve monitors the entries by each bank's ACH operators and reports no recurring procedural or coding errors. Errors are a result of mis-coding a name or number.

Lessons Learned:

Brown's suggestions center around aesthetics. This was a quick and clean job aid that worked. Brown believes that larger type would have made the job aid easier to read and that a graphic would have made the cover more interesting.

Example 2

ACG Networking Job Aid: The Alexander Consulting Group, Inc.

Need:

New employees at Alexander Consulting Group had difficulty directing potential clients to the appropriate service groups. Their one-hour orientation program was designed to address this need, but some new employees were unable to attend the program until one year after being hired. Others, even after attending the orientation, were unclear as to what services each department provided. During orientation, the leader distributed the company's organizational chart, described what the department did, and identified contact people. Patricia Patterson, Director, National Training, determined that a job aid would fulfill the following three needs: (1) to provide a better link between information and new employees' inquiries; (2) to provide information to those who were not able to attend orientation immediately after employment; and (3) to provide updated information to all employees.

Development:

This is an important example of how job aids can enhance the information flow in an organization and thus enable the organization to provide better service. To develop the job aid, Patterson asked the directors of each service area to provide three or four key words—

words most often used by clients—to describe their departments. Patterson spent about forty hours collecting information and developing this job aid. Most of that time was spent conducting needs assessments in preparation for the production of the information aid.

The job aid is a simple, print-based, decision-table format that employees are encouraged to slip under their desk blotters. Figure 7.2 shows a portion of the job aid that Patterson developed. Since it was first introduced, Patterson's job aid has been redeveloped and expanded from a one-page format to three pages. This illustration represents one page of the expanded version that appears in the company newsletter once each year with revisions and updates.

Delivery and Maintenance:

The job aid was designed to support the orientation program, but it easily could stand alone. In an orientation setting, the leader distributed the company's organizational chart and provided background for new hires. The job aid is used to emphasize relationships and connections between contact people and the services provided by their units. The orientation and the job aid are updated once each year. When a new employee is unable to attend the orientation, supervisors provide the employee with a copy of the job aid along with coaching on how to use it.

As mentioned earlier, some revisions are distributed via the company newsletter. Employees are responsible for updating their own job aids either by writing in the changes or using the updated versions that are published in the newsletter.

Impact:

New employees are able to direct clients to the appropriate service groups and contact people. Information about changes in available services and contact personnel is distributed much more efficiently. In addition to meeting the need for better information, the project introduced job-aid technology into the company.

Lessons Learned:

The development of this job aid illustrates the importance of matching informational job aids to the needs

If You Need Information on:	Then Contact:
• Data problems • Disclosure issues • PBGC • Records, procedures, forms	Benefits Administration George L. Huffman National Practice Director 125 Chubb Avenue Lyndhurst, New Jersey 07071 (201) 460-6700
• Employee surveys • Employee attitude research • Flex surveys	Employee Research Consulting G. Theodore Nygreen National Practice Director 125 Chubb Avenue Lyndhurst, New Jersey 07071 (201) 460-6700
• Sales information • Prospecting • Cold calling • Sales training	Client Development Program Rebecca West National Practice Director 125 Chubb Avenue Lyndhurst, New Jersey 07071 (201) 460-6700
• SPDs • Audiovisuals • Employee communications • Employee enrollment practices	Communications Consulting Services 300 East Joppa Road Baltimore, Maryland 21204 (301) 296-5500
• Interactive video • Providing direct access to benefit information • Helping employees make benefit decisions	Interactive Communications Services Jay L. Merchant National Practice Director 300 East Joppa Road Baltimore, Maryland 21204 (301) 296-5500

Figure 7.2. Decision Table Job Aid for Directing Clients to Appropriate Services

of end users. In this case the problems were the following: (1) the use of documentation that did not provide the end user with a clear understanding of the relationship among functional department, services available, and the contact person for each service group; (2) the employee's inability to attend orientation; and (3) changing services and contacts. New employees needed to be able to identify the clients' needs quickly and efficiently direct them to the most appropriate service provider. This job aid provided the information necessary to support that chain of events.

Patterson teaches job-aid development to other groups within the organization. She finds that many, especially those who develop manuals and documen-

tation, can use job aids to improve performance. She offered one caution. When teaching subject-matter experts how to develop job aids, she is careful to emphasize that job-aid development is not an intuitive process. She states, "It's an analytical process. Don't skip steps; be sure to break the job or task into its smallest parts before taking a crack at developing the job aid."

The introduction of a useful and friendly job aid firmly planted the notion that the Alexander Consulting Group can improve service by developing and using job aids.

Example 3

Port-A-Cath:
Robert Wood Johnson University Hospital

Need:

The Robert Wood Johnson University Hospital developed a job aid because nurses were trained to use a Port-A-Cath one year prior to the actual implementation of this new surgically inserted device. When the Port-A-Cath was introduced into the work setting, nurses did not remember what equipment they needed or how to change the needle and dressing. Nurses either had to review long complicated documentation or had to ask the clinical specialist to show them what equipment to use and how to use it. In addition, patients needed to know how to change their needles and dressings because they would be returning home with Port-A-Cath equipment.

Greg Finnegan, working with a clinical supervisor, determined that the need was for simple and accessible information about the Port-A-Cath for nurses and patients.

Development:

This is an example of what careful planning and dialog between performance professionals and line personnel can accomplish. Finnegan worked with the clinical supervisor and the head nurse to conduct a needs assessment for what became an eleven-page job aid. The head nurse and clinical supervisor invested five hours each outlining the content for the job.

aid, while Finnegan, with the help of a college student working as graphic artist, spent about five hours designing and developing the job aid.

The job aid relies on a checklist format. There are neither steps to follow nor clear-cut answers as to what to do or where to go when a piece of equipment is missing. It reminds the user that the equipment needs to be opened on a sterile barrier. This job aid provides an organized frame of reference for nurses and patients to determine whether they have all the equipment needed to change the needle and dressing on the Port-A-Cath. It is printed on card stock, is laminated, and is spiral bound. Figure 7.3 illustrates the job aid that Finnegan and his staff developed.

Delivery and Maintenance:

This job aid is given to nurses during an in-service course. The clinical supervisor reviews the information with the nurses and then encourages them to review the job aid prior to changing the needle and dressing on a Port-A-Cath. The clinical supervisor placed two job aids at each of eight locations throughout the hospital where Port-A-Cath devices are used.

About eight months after the implementation of this job aid, a similar one was developed for patients and/or family members. The patient or family member was given the job aid during an important training

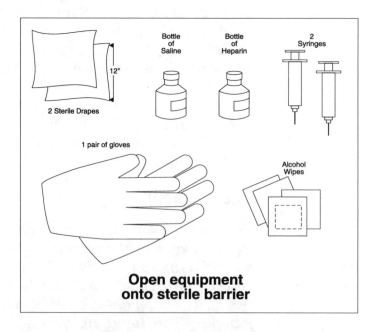

Figure 7.3. Checklist Job Aid for Port-A-Cath Procedures

session. He or she was supervised while practicing changing the needle and dressing.

This job aid is now used as part of orientation for new nurses.

Impact:

The job aid enabled nurses, patients, and family members to act independently. It replaced a one-hundred-page manual and reminded everyone of the critical need to perform all procedures related to the Port-A-Cath in a sterile environment.

Lessons Learned:

This informational job aid illustrates the beauty and cost effectiveness of a simple solution. It also reveals how effective job aids can work themselves out of a job. Because the Port-A-Cath is commonly used today, most nurses, patients, and family members do not need the job aid for very long. But the job aid will always play an important role in the lives of new nurses, new patients, and their families.

Example 4

Default Programmable Function (PF) Key Settings for Mainframe Computer System: Intel Corporation

Need:

Intel Corporation needed system users to achieve speedy proficiency on a new version of a software system. Diane McKinnon, the Information-Systems Training-Program Manager, determined that the goal was consistent and immediate use of programmable function (PF) keys for navigation throughout the system.

Development:

McKinnon reported that a designer, a subject-matter expert, and a computer-systems expert collaborated on the development of this job aid. The job aid was then produced using desktop publishing on a Xerox system. It took about four hours to develop seven of these job aids, a different one for each functional group. The combined development cost for these job *aids was approximately one hundred dollars. The job aid was also programmed into the system in the form of help screens at the time the new system software was developed. (The cost of the help screens is not included in the one-hundred-dollar development cost.)*

The job aid relies on a reference-table (array) format. Based on the needed function or screen, the user is directed to the appropriate function key. For example, Figure 7.4 shows a portion of this job aid. An Indirect-Materials Planner/Buyer who wants to go to the "NEXT" screen must press "PF6." However, a Document-Control-Center user who wants to go to the "NEXT" screen must press "PF10."

This job aid is delivered through print. Five job aids were copied on an 8½" x 11" piece of colored card stock. Each job aid was then cut into separate strips.

Delivery and Maintenance:

Although this job-aid information is readily available on-line, McKinnon and her staff believe that employees tend to rely on the printed job aid rather than on switching to another screen to search for information. The printed version of this job aid is delivered as part of a course during which the instructor provides a brief explanation and demonstration.

Updates to the system, training, and job aids are initiated every three years. The plan is to develop and distribute color-coded updates that correspond to the cover of the most recent system manual.

Impact:

"They used them!" Class participants liked using the job aids in the class and asked for extras to take back to their work sites. Once they were back on the job, new users were able to operate the new system.

Lessons Learned:

This job aid illustrates using job aids to support new systems. McKinnon reported that she would not change a thing. "The job aid was popular, cheap, and easy to produce. And it worked."

intel

Indirect Materials Planner/Buyer - iMACS II PF Key Settings

PF1:	PITM	PF2:	PLIT	PF3:	DELS	PF4:	SSIT
PF5:	SDDQ	PF6:	NEXT	PF7:	PAGB	PF8:	PAGF
PF9:	PREV	PF10:	RSET	PF11:	POIT	PF12:	MD00

intel

Stores - iMACS II PF Key Settings

PF1:	HELP	PF2:	IADJ	PF3:	MOVO	PF4:	MATM
PF5:	ISSM	PF6:	RECO	PF7:	PAGB	PF8:	PAGF
PF9:	PREV	PF10:	NEXT	PF11:	SSIT	PF12:	ITHQ

intel

Document Control Center - iMACS II PF Key Settings

PF1:	HELP	PF2:	ITEM	PF3:	REV	PF4:	TEXT
PF5:	BREQ	PF6:	WU	PF7:	PAGB	PF8:	PAGF
PF9:	MD00	PF10:	TM	PF11:	AM	PF12:	SO

intel

Planner/Buyer - iMACS II PF Key Settings

PF1:	MD00	PF2:	SDDQ	PF3:	PURM	PF4:	PCON
PF5:	PORD	PF6:	DELS	PF7:	PAGB	PF8:	PAGF
PF9:	PREV	PF10:	NEXT	PF11:	POIT	PF12:	SSIT

Figure 7.4. Array Job Aid for PF Key Settings

Review of Examples of Job Aids for Informing

This chapter illustrates how four professionals used job aids to solve four different but typical needs for information.

Denise Brown, in the Commercial-Services Development department at Sovran Bank, provided a job aid that supplied new codes and terminology to Automated Clearing House (ACH) employees. The experienced employee was given the job aid with minimal direction, and the two new employees received the job aid during new-employee training. Because there were only three work stations in the ACH department, Denise ensured that a job aid was available at each workstation. The Federal Reserve reports that there are no recurring coding or procedural errors. The problem was solved for just one hundred dollars.

Patricia Patterson, Director, National Training, for the Alexander Consulting Group, Inc., relied on job aids as a primary method for providing information to new employees about each service group's function, its relationship to the needs of the client, and the contact person within the group. In addition, the job aid was used to alert all employees to changes in services and contact people. This job aid demonstrates how job aids can improve client service and internal information flow.

Greg Finnegan, Director, Management Systems for The Robert Wood Johnson University Hospital, developed a job aid that served a number of needs: (1) it provided information to refresh the skills of nurses who had received training on the Port-A-Cath a year prior to its actual use, and (2) it provided information to support new nurse and patient training. This experience illustrates how job aids can evolve to meet the needs of many end-users. In addition, job aids can be used to support refresher training and to support new users when learning a new process that will, in time, become second nature.

Diane McKinnon, Information-Systems Training-Program Manager for Intel Corporation, needed to provide assistance to help users of a new system. McKinnon developed a print job aid in addition to the "PF" key function information that was on-line. During needs assessment, McKinnon found that users were more accustomed to print and not inclined to switch back and forth between screens to use the on-line system. For one hundred dollars and about four hours' work, McKinnon and her staff developed a set of job aids that enabled users to get up to speed quickly on the new system.

Job Aids for Informing

Job aids for informing are used to answer questions about who, what, which, and where. They are most often seen in the forms of checklists and decision tables but may also appear as or in combination with work sheets and flow charts In addition, job aids for informing are often presented as on-line computer help systems, on paper, and through posters.

Review of Chapter 7

Job Aids for Informing Are Needed When:

- The performer needs information;
- The performance is infrequent or new;
- The consequences of error are high;
- The situation is complex;
- The job or organization is changing, and employees need to do their work differently;
- There is no need to memorize information; or
- There are insufficient resources for training.

Job Aids for Informing Use These Formats:

- Checklist;
- Decision Table;
- Work Sheet; or
- Flow Chart.

Job Aids for Informing Use These Media and Packaging:

- Laminated paper with color highlights;
- Paper with spiral binding;
- Paper with glue binding (such as a telephone book);
- A strip of colored card stock;
- Laminated paper, spiral bound and tented;
- Paper/card stock, packaged with training and separately;
- Poster sized; or
- On-line.

Job Aids for Informing Use These Mechanisms for Delivery and Maintenance:

- Stand alone at the work station and are revised regularly;
- Provide information used in the training course;

- Support training exercises;
- Are delivered with software and user manuals;
- Are used during training and to support on-the-job performance;
- Are posted on the wall;
- Provide help screens or imbedded prompts; or
- Provide information for work sheets.

Job Aids for Informing Have These Impacts:

- Result in no recurring coding errors;
- Enable use of a new system;
- Improve the flow of information;
- Improve customer service;
- Enable independent work; and
- Alert users to critical information.

Job Aids for Informing Result in These Lessons Learned:

- Use graphics when appropriate;
- Develop job aids that create a link between information and the user's need for that information;
- Consider and document the cost/benefit of using job aids;
- Collaborate with line employees and field test the job aid early in the development process;
- Enable others in the organization to develop job aids;
- Provide only the most essential information;
- Consider others who may find the job aid useful; and
- If the job aid works, do not change it.

Preview of Chapter 8

Chapter 8 provides examples and commentaries about "real-world" job aids that support procedures.

Job Aids for Procedures

Chapter 8 provides examples of how job aids support procedures. In addition, extensive interviews with the people who created and used these job aids resulted in commentaries on what worked, how it worked, and what the creators now would do differently. This chapter begins with a brief reiteration of the definition of job aids that support procedures, followed by five examples and commentaries.

Defining Job Aids That Support Procedures

Job aids that support procedures tell and show actions, order, and results. Effective procedural job aids answer questions about when to use the job aid and how to do the job or task. Procedural job aids emphasize action steps in order and often show action paired with results, so that the user can evaluate the work.

Examples of Job Aids for Procedures

The following pages provide five examples of job aids that address typical needs for procedures.

Example 1

Seal Ring Installation:
Caterpillar Tractor, Inc.

Need:

Caterpillar Tractor developed a job aid because a particular portion of a product was not passing quality control. The back-up ring and seal were not being properly installed. Line management, working with Barry Boothe in the training department, determined that the cause of the problem was inappropriate performance by new and/or temporary employees.

Development:

This is an example of what careful planning by performance professionals and the line can accomplish. Boothe reported that one designer and one illustrator collaborated on the development of this job aid and that it cost only a few hundred dollars. The job aid relies on a step format and is delivered through print. It is laminated, includes color, and was reproduced on a color copier. Figure 8.1 shows the job aid that Boothe and his staff developed.

Delivery and Maintenance:

Training staff placed the job aid on a flat area of the assembly benches. In some cases, the job aid was attached to the wall near the work station.

Caterpillar Tractor uses quality work teams, including engineers, trainers, operators, and so on, to examine performance and to consider how current job aids are as well as to consider the usefulness of job aids. This is a situation in which the operators have a history of comfort with and reliance on job aids. Employees are so dependent on the job aids and are so pleased with these aids that they ask for updates and carefully maintain current versions of their support tools. Boothe tells a story about a new water cooler be-

ing delivered; soon after, an employee with a sense of humor called to ask why no job aid accompanied the water cooler.

Impact:

The job aid to support the seal-ring installing procedure enabled new and temporary employees to perform the task as necessary.

Lessons Learned:

This job aid illustrates the importance of collaboration between line employees and supervisors. It also describes the possibility of creating a culture in an organization in which employees identify opportunities for job aids and support and maintain them once they have been introduced.

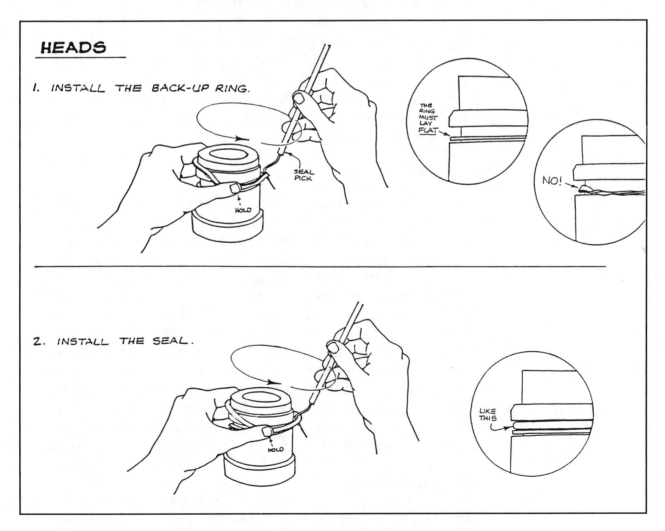

Figure 8.1. Step Job Aid for Assembling Back-Up Rings and Seals

Example 2

E.1 Turn On Machine and Access AMCISS Main Menu: Performance Engineering Network, Inc.

Need:

Workers at the Army Materiel Command found themselves unable to operate a new computer system that was to enable them to process supply orders on-line rather than on paper. Not surprisingly, the Army logistics personnel, many of whom had no previous experience using computers, were unable to use the 720-page documentation to operate the system. Working with Donald Mitchell and Michele Schulman from Performance Engineering Network, Inc., the Army determined that the cause of the problem was inadequate training and documentation/job aids and replaced the existing materials with a series of job aids from which this example is drawn. In addition, the Army wanted the new documentation/job aids to provide structure for a course that would diminish resistance to the new system and support people as they learned how to use it.

Development:

This is an example of how job aids, combined with training, can enhance the integration of a new computer system and improve performance. To develop the 291-page job aid (which included forty-eight task-specific job aids), Mitchell worked with a committee of three Army logistics experts. Each expert was adept at processing orders using the old system; one was computer literate, one was keyboard literate, and one was computer and keyboard illiterate. Mitchell and the committee worked for six weeks to complete their analysis. Two developers then worked for four months to develop the job aids, and a graphic artist added an additional fifty hours of time. The two developers spent one month validating this extensive procedural job aid. In all, the development cost was approximately $60,000.

The job aid relies on a step format and is delivered through print. It is bound in a three-inch loose-leaf binder, which is indexed and tabbed by duty.

Figure 8.2 shows one page from the 291-page job aid that Mitchell and his staff developed.

Delivery and Maintenance:

The job aid was used to guide the training of a sampling of the "real-world" population. The training focused on how to use the table of contents and included opportunities to use the job aids with on-line practice exercises. Trained logistics personnel then returned to the field and trained everyone else. The Army relies heavily on training as a means to introduce new procedures and systems. Mitchell described what happened when he first introduced the idea of developing job aids to replace the existing documentation and to diminish the need for training. At first, the program manager was vehemently against the idea. He wanted people trained so that their skills were stored in long-term memory. Mitchell, however, presented a good case for using job aids instead of training. He estimated cost (20 percent less to develop job aids) and risks (shipping the wrong item), which helped the project manager settle on a combination of training and job aids. As a result, Mitchell developed forty-eight job aids that were used to guide the training. The training was reduced from twenty-five days to six hours at enormous savings. In addition, veteran employees were given an opportunity, in a controlled environment, to see the electronic system as easy, now that it was supported by new documentation/job aids.

Mitchell speaks to the project manager regularly and has learned that the on-line supply system has had many updates. Unfortunately, there have been no formal updates to the job aids. Because the project manager says that the job aids are still helping, Mitchell speculates that logistics personnel are updating the job aids themselves. Another possibility is that because the system is used so frequently, people have "learned" the computer system and the aids are no longer necessary.

Impact:

The project manager reports that the job-aids approach worked. The job aid enabled all Army logistics personnel to operate the new on-line supply system.

E.6 Query Data

Researching information can be done in a number of ways. Using the Inquiry function available in the computer may save you some time and effort. Go ahead and try it, you may like it!

Step 1:   Enter the Main Menu if you are not there now.

Step 2:   Enter your installation code.

Step 3:   Enter [3], then [0], then [0], then [0],

in the   ENTER SELECTION=> _____ .

Step 4:   Then Press [Return]

You will see <<wait>> in the lower right corner of the screen.

Then this will be on your screen:

```
HDBD01                    A M C I S S
11:03:02          INQUIRY/OUTPUT SUBMENU-3000         10 NOV 1991
---------------------------------------------------------------

        3100      ASSETS AND LOCATIONS INQUIRY
        3200      INVENTORY RESEARCH INQUIRY
        3300      AMC ISA MASTER FILE INQUIRIES (ON-LINE)
        3400      MANAGEMENT INFORMATION SYSTEM INQUIRIES
        3500      MASS INQUIRIES (BATCH)
---------------------------------------------------------------
 F3=EXIT                              ENTER SELECTION>=_____
 ENTER SELECTION AND PRESS ENTER
```

Figure 8.2. Step Job Aid for Query Data

Lessons Learned:

The combination of job aids and training illustrates the importance of identifying all the needs of end users. In this case, the problem was not only a lack of skills and knowledge because of poor documentation but also a lack of confidence about the ability to use the system. During practice exercises, the Army used a live data bed that was the part of the mainframe holding the "real" supply numbers. This saved money because the Army avoided developing a test bed. Having access to the live data bed during training, however, was dangerous. The introduction of user-friendly documentation/job aids firmly planted the idea that job aids have a role to play in supporting procedures.

Example 3

Cost-Justification Work Sheet and Job Aid: Wells Fargo Bank

Need:

Wells Fargo developed a job aid as part of a production-management course to enable service managers to turn good ideas into cost-saving programs. The job aid was built because service managers sought a convenient way to quantify the potential cost savings associated with new ideas. The following story explains the problem. In the past, a service manager who had a great idea would approach the branch manager and say something like "We need a new copy machine." The branch manager would respond, "You'll have to justify the cost." The service manager would wonder, "How can I justify it?" The branch manager would explain, "Well, let me look at the dollars." Not knowing how to turn an idea into a visual, cost-justified plan, the service manager would usually drop the idea. Wells Fargo saw an opportunity to help managers achieve their goals and acquire new skills.

Development:

Careful planning and dialog between performance professionals and the line can accomplish a great deal. Wells Fargo's Retail Staff-Development department worked with Darlene Frank and Associates, an external consulting company, in the development of the course that contained this job aid and many others.

The job aid has two parts. Part A relies on a work-sheet format; Part B uses a step format to portray the overall procedure for using the work sheet. It is printed on a double-sized sheet of paper and is bound in a three-ring loose-leaf binder. Figure 8.3 shows a portion of the job aid that was developed.

Delivery and Maintenance:

This procedural job aid was given to service managers during a production-development course. The job aid was used to complete a management-development activity in which managers determined the current cost and proposed savings for a program they wanted to

COST JUSTIFICATION WORK SHEET   Project _____   Svc. Mgr. _____

CURRENT COST

1. Calculate labor costs for each employee:

Emp #1
HRS/WK ON TASK	=	___	A
HOURLY SALARY	=$	___	B
BENEFITS @ 30%	=$	___	C
A x [B+C] x 52 WKS	=$	___	D

Emp #2
HRS/WK ON TASK	=	___	A
HOURLY SALARY	=$	___	B
BENEFITS @ 30%	=$	___	C
A x [B+C] x 52 WKS	=$	___	D

ADD ALL D's TO CALCULATE
TOTAL ANNUAL LABOR $ ___ E

2. Calculate supplies cost for all supplies used in the task that must be replaced. Do not calculate if current proposed costs are the same:

ITEM #1
QUANTITY USED/WK	=$	___	A
ITEM COST	=$	___	B
A x B x 52 WKS	=$	___	C

ITEM #2
QUANTITY USED/WK	=$	___	A
ITEM COST	=$	___	B
A x B x 52 WKS	=$	___	C

TOTAL ANNUAL SUPPLIES $ ___ E

3. Calculate cost of equipment rental, lease, and maintenance only if equipment will not be used in proposed costs:

ITEM #1
ANNUAL COST $ ___ A
ITEM #2
ANNUAL COST $ ___ A

TOTAL ANNUAL EQUIP/MAINT $ ___ E

PROPOSED COST (AFTER)

1. Calculate proposed labor costs:

Emp #1
HRS/WK ON TASK	=	___	A
HOURLY SALARY	=$	___	B
BENEFITS @ 30%	=$	___	C
A x [B+C] x 52 WKS	=$	___	D

Emp #2
HRS/WK ON TASK	=	___	A
HOURLY SALARY	=$	___	B
BENEFITS @ 30%	=$	___	C
A x [B+C] x 52 WKS	=$	___	D

ADD ALL D's TO CALCULATE
TOTAL ANNUAL LABOR $ ___ G

2. Calculate proposed supplies cost:

ITEM #1
QUANTITY USED/WK	=$	___	A
ITEM COST	=$	___	B
A x B x 52 WKS	=$	___	C

ITEM #2
QUANTITY USED/WK	=$	___	A
ITEM COST	=$	___	B
A x B x 52 WKS	=$	___	C

TOTAL ANNUAL SUPPLIES $ ___ G

3. Calculate proposed equipment cost:

ITEM #1
ANNUAL COST $ ___ A
ITEM #2
ANNUAL COST $ ___ A

TOTAL ANNUAL EQUIP/MAINT $ ___ G

CURRENT COST(BEFORE)

4. Calculate operating costs for items such as postage, rent, utilities, computer time, cross-charges:

ITEM #1
WEEKLY USAGE	=$	___	A
ITEM COST	=$	___	B
A x B x 52 WKS	=$	___	C

ITEM #2
WEEKLY USAGE	=$	___	A
ITEM COST	=$	___	B
A x B x 52 WKS	=$	___	C

TOTAL ANNUAL SUPPLIES $ ___ E

6. Total current costs:
Add all the E Figures:
TOTAL ANNUAL LABOR	$ ___	A
TOTAL ANNUAL SUPPLIES	$ ___	B
TOTAL ANNUAL EQUIP.	$ ___	C
TOTAL ANNUAL OPER.	$ ___	

TOTAL CURRENT COSTS: $ ___ F

7. ANNUAL NET SAVINGS
Calculate the difference between the current and proposed total costs:
F =$ ___
H =$ ___
F minus H =$ ___   Annual Net Savings

Determine hard and soft dollar costs:
Hard $ savings =$ ___
Soft $ savings =$ ___

PROPOSED COST (AFTER)

4. Calculate proposed operating costs:

ITEM #1
WEEKLY USAGE	=$	___	A
ITEM COST	=$	___	B
A x B x 52 WKS	=$	___	C

ITEM #2
WEEKLY USAGE	=$	___	A
ITEM COST	=$	___	B
A x B x 52 WKS	=$	___	C

TOTAL ANNUAL SUPPLIES $ ___ G

5. Calculate one-time costs for construction, moving, and new equipment:

ITEM #1
ONE-TIME COST $ ___ A
ITEM #2
ONE-TIME COST $ ___ A

TOTAL ONE-TIME COST $ ___ G

6. Total proposed costs:
Add all the G Figures:
TOTAL ANNUAL LABOR $ ___
TOTAL ANNUAL SUPPLIES $ ___
TOTAL ANNUAL EQUIP. $ ___
TOTAL ANNUAL OPER. $ ___
TOTAL ONE-TIME COSTS $ ___
TOTAL PROPOSED COSTS $ ___ H

Figure 8.3 (Part A). Step and Work-Sheet Job Aid for Cost Justification

COMPLETING THE COST JUSTIFICATION WORK SHEET	
Step	**Action**
1	Complete the project information at the top of the form: • Project title • Your name
2	Calculate current costs first: • Complete requested information for current labor costs. • Calculate total labor costs using the work-sheet formula. • Enter the total labor cost at E on the work sheet.
3	Complete calculations for supplies, equipment rental, and operating costs by following the instructions and formulas on the work sheet.
4	Total all current costs in box 6 at F.
5	Calculate all proposed cost figures for labor, supplies, equipment, operating costs, and one-time costs. Enter the total cost for each item at G in each box.
6	Total all proposed costs in box 6 at H.
7	Calculate the annual net savings using the formula in box 7. Break out Hard and Soft dollar amounts for this first figure and enter in the space provided.

**Figure 8.3 (Part B). Step and Work-Sheet
Job Aid for Cost Justification**

implement in their branches. Managers, working with Retail Staff-Development, determined that the job aid needed to appear nontechnical, to use a large font, and to offer plenty of white space for calculations. In addition, the job aid needed to fit on one page so that the user would not need to flip pages. This job aid treats stable content and does not require updates. Each service manager was given ten copies of the form and was encouraged to reproduce it as needed.

Impact:

The job aid was a complete success. Currently service managers who use it have been able to prove significant savings to upper management. In addition, when the job aid was brought back to the branches, many branch managers asked for copies of the job aid and instructions for its use.

Lessons Learned:

Listening to the needs of the end users kept the development team from falling into traps. One might assume that people who work with numbers would be comfortable only with a numbers-oriented work sheet. On the contrary, the managers were pleased that the job aid consisted of familiar words and that the entries progressed from common-knowledge calculations like salaries to other accessible items like equipment costs. Feedback comments like "Make the print bigger!" and "Put it all on one page!" were invaluable, though contradictory.

Example 4

CENTURYNET ® : Quick Reference to Prospecting: Sales and Listing: Century 21 Real Estate Corporation

Need:

This procedural job aid was developed by Century 21 Real Estate Corporation to assist in the implementation of an automated real estate system. CENTURY 21 sales brokers operate independent businesses; when a new system is introduced, each broker chooses whether or not to make the purchase. Century 21 Real Estate Corporation's international headquarters provides software, support, and training. During the initial implementation of this new system, it became apparent that employees needed extensive training and job aids in order for the system to be effective. Dana Bruttig, whose department was responsible for training and documentation, worked with an external contractor and found the following problems: (1) the system did not use intuitive commands; (2) sales associates had little or no computer literacy; and (3) many critical functions were infrequently used.

Development:

Century 21 Real Estate Corporation invested significant resources to ensure that this new system was properly supported with training and documentation.

Bruttig reports that one designer and one subject-matter expert/instructional designer, together with an external graphic-arts company, collaborated on the development of this job aid. The development cost was approximately three thousand dollars, and the production cost for each job aid was three dollars. Figure 8.4 shows one page of the full ten-page (double-sided) job aid.

The procedural job aid relies on a steps format and is delivered through print. It is laminated, spiral bound, and tented so that sales associates can place it next to the computer. This job aid has two purposes. When opened on one side, it is the job aid for "Quick Reference to Prospecting." When it is opened from the other direction, it is the job aid for the CenturyWriter®, the word-processing function.

TELEMARKETING

The CENTURYNET® CALL function is available whenever you are viewing a Client or Property Profile. The computer will dial a number that is contained in either the Home or Business Telephone fields of a Client Profile, or the Phone field of a Property Profile. Below are the steps to take when you want to call everyone in a select group of Clients or Properties.

STEP ONE: Select Sales & Listing Package at the Main Menu.

STEP TWO: To initiate calls to a client group, select Client Follow-up. For calls to a property group, select Farming.

STEP THREE: Select the Group Profile function on the menu.

STEP FOUR: Type the name of your group and press Enter. The name you typed will appear at the top of a page of group names if the Group Profile exists. (See "Create a Group" to define a new Group Profile.)

STEP FIVE: With the highlight bar on your selected group name, press Enter. The group criteria screen will appear.

STEP SIX: To view the first profile in the group, type V (for REVIEW).

STEP SEVEN: With the profile in view, type C (for CALL).

STEP EIGHT: The CALL function displays the phone numbers in the profile and also provides a field for you to enter a different number. Select one of the numbers for the computer to dial. To select, type the digit 1, 2, or 3 that corresponds to the telephone number.

STEP NINE: When the call is complete, you may add comments about the conversation to the phone activity entry made in the Client Contact Log. If the call did not complete, select RESCHEDULE to ensure this call will be included in a tickler list. Press the F10 key to exit the CALL function.

Figure 8.4. Step Job Aid for Real Estate Prospecting

Delivery and Maintenance:

Initially, the job aid was delivered as part of class-room training. Now self-paced computer-based train-ing and job aids are mailed to new users of the hardware and software.

The company gathers and analyzes data from its Telephone Help Desk. Systems engineers and the training unit use these data to make changes to the system, training, and job aids. The CENTURY 21® system initiates updates one or two times each year. The system distributes updates and collects old ver-sions of all software and training materials through Regional Automation Consultants. The Regional Auto-mation Consultant is also responsible for installing new and updated software, for providing one-on-one training when requested, and for running monthly system checks to determine how frequently the sys-tem is used.

Impact:

Bruttig judges the success of the job aids through the feedback received from the Telephone Help Desk—the fewer the calls, the better the job aid is working. In addition, the data received from the monthly system checks show that those who have purchased systems are using them.

Lessons Learned:

This job aid illustrates the importance of high-level corporate support for job aids and training. Providing quality training and job aids proved to brokers and sales associates that the CENTURY 21® organization stood behind its systems. Bruttig had difficulty look-ing at the "Quick Reference to Prospecting" job aid in isolation. When asked what she would do differently, she mentioned integrating the job aids into the total training system. She said she would have made greater reference to the job aids in the computer-based training. For example, a system prompt could have read, "Now you are ready to begin telemarketing your prospects. Turn to Section 2 in the 'Quick Refer-ence to Prospecting.'"

In all, the job aids worked. They helped sales associates to feel confident that the vast amounts of information needed to do the job were only a glance away. CENTURY 21 brokers and sales associates appreciated being able to place their job aids next to their terminals and begin working.

Example 5

Computing Per Diem: The Mitchell Group

Need:

The Mitchell Group developed this job aid for travel-voucher examiners (clerical staff) who worked at the United States Department of State. The procedure for processing travel-expense vouchers is very complex. The Department of State sought help because the examiners were making many errors, resulting in frustration and, consequently, high turnover. Line management, working with Andrea Mitchell from The Mitchell Group, established that this was a performance problem that could be solved through training and documentation.

Development:

This is an example of how the development of job aids encourages developers to think logically about work flow from both macro and micro perspectives. Mitchell described how this particular job aid naturally fell out of the needs-assessment and development processes. "Computing Per Diem" was not "planned." However, in the process of developing the job aids for the travel-expense portion of the training, the developers realized that an overview procedural job aid was needed. Mitchell reported that one project manager, one designer, and two subject-matter experts collaborated on the development of this project, which included many job aids. This particular job aid took one designer (Kathy Reardon) less than one-half day to develop and cost only a few hundred dollars. The job aid relies on a flow-chart format, is delivered through print, and is printed on card stock. Figure 8.5 depicts the job aid that Mitchell and her staff developed.

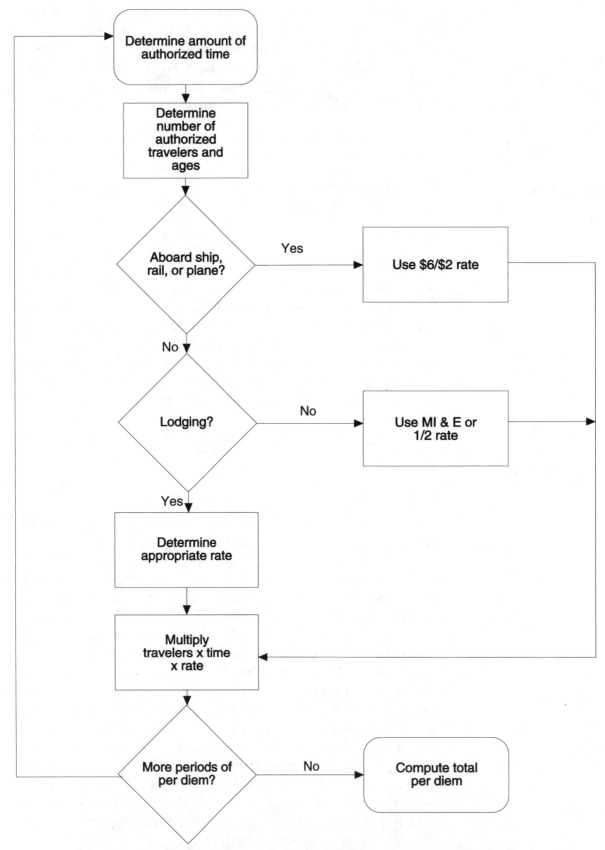

Figure 8.5. Flow-Chart Job Aid for Computing Per Diem

Delivery and Maintenance:

The aid was delivered as part of mandatory training for all existing and new voucher examiners in the United States Department of State. It was included as part of the training materials and also in a separately packaged card-stock version for easy use on the job. The Department of State relies on supervisors to evaluate performance. The supervisors are responsible for training new clerical employees and for keeping existing employees up-to-date on new procedures. Prior to the Department of State's request for outside support, the supervisors relied on a system of informal on-the-job training, not supported by job aids at all. When Mitchell began to develop the training and job aids, the supervisors were skeptical about the claims of fewer errors, increased efficiency, lower turnover, and increased morale. Supervisors served first as subject-matter experts and ultimately as the trainers/job-aid deliverers. Soon after the completion of the first training course, the supervisors were amazed by the results.

Impact:

The training that was supported by job aids was piloted in February, 1990. No empirical data are available at this time, but anecdotal evidence suggests a marked improvement in performance. In addition, Mitchell reports the travel-expense vouchers that were previously backlogged have been brought up to date.

Review of Examples of Job Aids for Procedures

This chapter illustrates how five professionals used job aids to solve five different, but typical, procedural problems.

Barry Boothe, a training manager, provided a job aid to help new and temporary employees assemble rings and seals on equipment heads to ensure quality control. His organization could not support all employees' receiving individual training or feedback on how to install the rings and seals. Boothe needed a quick solution for reducing the number of scrapped heads. Job aids offered ready access to the steps for properly installing rings and seals as well as information on recognizing incorrect installation. Because rings and seals were installed at only a few work stations, Boothe used color-highlighted printed job aids and ensured that one was available at each work station.

Don Mitchell and Michele Schulman, training consultants with Performance Engineering Network, Inc., developed steps job aids for Army logistics personnel to use when operating a new automated supply-processing system. In addition to providing training and on-the-job support to employees, job aids demonstrated to supervisors how improved documentation/job aids could minimize resistance to the change from a paper-based to an automated system.

Roger Addison, Vice President and Manager for Retail Staff-Development at Wells Fargo Bank, developed a tool for service managers to use when considering the costs and benefits of implementing new programs. As an organization that emphasizes quality and employee participation, Wells Fargo turned to job aids to help managers handle a key challenge, the process of justifying the costs of new programs and ideas.

Dana Bruttig, then a training manager for Century 21 Real Estate Corporation, used procedural job aids to help real estate personnel use a new automated real estate system. The problem was that sales associates, for the most part, had no experience in using computers, and the system that was developed did not speak in "real estate language." Using self-paced training and job aids, new sales associates were able to operate the system and to complete critical tasks for selling real estate.

Andrea Mitchell used job aids to support training for voucher examiners at the United States Department of State. The "Computing per Diem" job aid shown in Figure 8.5 uses a flow-chart format and was designed to provide an overview of the process for computing per-diem expenses. In addition to supporting training and providing on-the-job support for employees, the process of job-aid development helped supervisors to perceive the value of a systematic approach.

Job Aids for Procedures

Job aids for procedures are used to help people complete a job or task with confidence. They fulfill the same needs as all other job aids and accomplish the same results. They are most often seen in the form of steps and work-sheet job aids but may also appear as or in combination with flow-chart and decision-table job aids. In addition, job aids for procedures are often presented on paper. Other media well suited for job aids for procedures are posters, on-line computer help systems, and audio coaches.

Review of Chapter 8

Job Aids for Procedures Are Needed When:

- The performance is a procedure;
- The performance is infrequent;
- The consequences of error are high;
- The situation is complex;
- The job or organization is changing and employees need to do their work differently;
- There is no need to memorize steps; or
- There are insufficient resources for training.

Job Aids for Procedures Use These Formats:

- Step;
- Work Sheet;
- Decision Table; or
- Flow Chart.

Job Aids for Procedures Use These Media and Packaging:

- Laminated paper with color highlights;
- Paper bound in a three-ring binder;
- Double-sized sheets of paper, bound in a three-ring binder;
- Laminated paper, spiral bound and tented;
- Paper/card stock, packaged with training and packaged separately;
- Poster sized;
- On-line; or
- Audio.

Job Aids for Procedures Use These Mechanisms for Delivery and Maintenance:

- Stand-alone format, placed at work station, with automatic updates with new procedures or equipment;
- As structure for the training course;

- As support for training activities;
- Delivered with software, with self-paced computer-based training and automatic updates once or twice yearly;
- Used during training and used to support on-the-job performance;
- Posted on the wall;
- As help screens or imbedded prompts; or
- As structure for work sheets.

Job Aids for Procedures Have These Impacts:

- Improved performance of employees;
- Quicker integration of new systems;
- Ability to use new systems;
- Increased profit and/or savings for the organization;
- Decrease in employees' errors;
- Increased employee confidence; and
- Development of collaborative habits between developers and line personnel.

Job Aids for Procedures Result in These Lessons Learned:

- A culture can be created in which employees see opportunities for job aids;
- The cost benefits of using job aids need to be considered and documented;
- Collaboration with line employees and field testing job aids early in the development stage is important;
- The bigger picture need to be considered when developing job aids for new systems; and
- Using flowcharts helps employees to visualize complex procedures.

Preview of Chapter 9

Chapter 9 provides examples of "real-world" job aids for decision making and coaching. This chapter provides useful examples from which training and development professionals can develop job aids to fit individual needs.

Job Aids for Decision Making and Coaching

Chapter 9 provides examples of job aids that support and coach decisions. In addition, extensive interviews with the people who created and used these job aids elicited their commentaries on what worked, how it worked, and what the creators now would do differently. This chapter begins with a brief review of the definition of heuristic job aids, aids that influence the way people approach their work and the decisions they are called on to make. Four examples are presented and discussed.

Defining Job Aids That Coach Perspectives and Support Decisions

Coaching or heuristic aids expand on the traditional uses of job aids by prompting the user regarding approaches, thoughts, and perspectives for undertaking a job. Effective heuristic job aids go beyond how to carry out a task to the details of what is involved in thinking about it. An effective way to promote self-evaluation of performance, heuristic aids can be important contributors before, during, and after performance.

This new kind of job aid is emerging in response to the following significant contemporary trends:

- A focus on how people prepare to face a challenge or capitalize on an opportunity;

- The recognition that human resource professionals have both an opportunity and a responsibility to influence how employees organize information, approach a task, and prepare to act;

- The belief that superior performance has roots in thoughts and speech and that both thoughts and speech can be influenced with guidelines and suggestions; and

- An emphasis on self-evaluation and quality control in organizations as a result of having fewer managers spread across many locations and miles.

Job aids have grown into tools that influence thoughts, feelings, and eventually effort and accomplishment. They do this by organizing subject matter and by creating mental models for approaching challenges, perspectives on jobs, and reasons for effort. The examples in this chapter illustrate these points.

Examples of Job Aids for Coaching Perspectives and Decisions

Example 1

The following pages provide four examples of job aids that address typical needs for coaching perspectives and supporting decisions.

Excavations & Trenches 5 FT or More Deep Must Be Shored or Sloped: General Telephone of California

Need:

General Telephone of California developed this job aid because too many accidents and near misses occurred as a result of improper and incautious ditch digging. Supervisors and workers needed to dig each ditch with certain important safety factors in mind. Existing documentation was contained in extensive manuals that were not available at work sites.

Supervisors worked with Bob Hobbs in the Education and Training Department and decided that workers needed reminders and ready access to documentation where and when they were faced with digging ditches. In addition, they recognized that all classroom training sessions needed to be infused with attention to safety.

Development:

General Telephone developed this job aid for three reasons: (1) to boost employees' skill and knowledge regarding safe ditch digging; (2) to hold workers accountable for safe excavations; and (3) to remind workers of ways to be vigilant regarding their own safety. Hobbs reports that two subject-matter experts, two course developers, and one graphic artist collaborated on the development of this job aid. The subject-matter experts each spent forty hours, and the course developers each spent twelve hours on it.

The job aid relies on an array format and is delivered through print. It is produced in color and is laminated on a 3" x 7" piece of paper. The job aid was designed to fit in a shirt pocket. Figure 9.1 shows the job aid that Hobbs and his staff developed.

Delivery and Maintenance:

This job aid is delivered in three ways: (1) during formal new-employee training; (2) during "tailgate" sessions (short training sessions that occur at the job site just prior to work); and (3) by posting it in an obvious place at the job site. For new-employee training, this job aid is bound with other similar job aids to form a pocket-sized pamphlet. During "tailgate" sessions, supervisors disseminate the job aids that they have received through the company mail, with cover letters explaining their links to safety. The supervisor demonstrates how to use the job aid, explains why it is important, and distributes laminated copies to employees. The supervisor also posts the job aid at the work site.

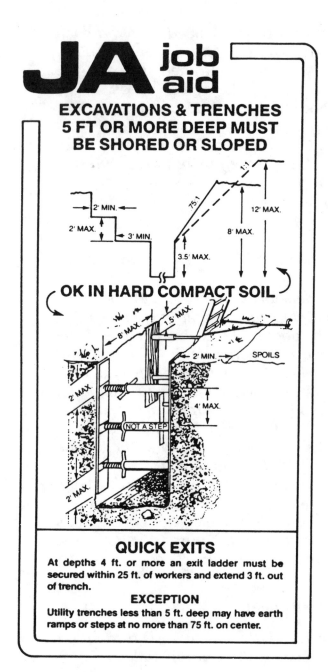

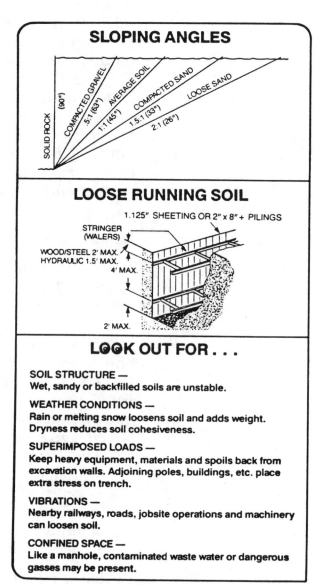

Figure 9.1. Array Job Aid for Excavations and Trenches

Construction and safety codes rarely change; therefore, Hobbs says, there is little need for updating this job aid.

Impact:

Hobbs reports that this job aid has reduced OSHA (Occupational Safety and Health Administration) and safety code violations. However, he cautions against at-

tributing all of the impact to the effect of the job aid. At the time of the introduction of the job aid, management simultaneously increased its emphasis on safety issues in training classes and performance reviews. The heuristic job aid was one component in a larger safety system.

Lessons Learned:

This job aid describes the importance of using job aids to support complete performance-improvement systems. Hobbs believes that this job aid effectively reminded employees how to dig ditches safely, stimulated safety consciousness, and encouraged employees to heed safety guidelines.

Hobbs concedes that if he could develop the job aids over again he would develop one job aid that covered the entire job rather than many task-specific job aids. He is concerned that an employee who receives twenty-five or thirty pocket-sized job aids will begin to lose interest and pocket space for them.

This job aid illustrates the importance of building a strong performance-support system to achieve organizational goals, a system in which job aids play a supporting role. Many things that the organization did, including producing the readily available job aid, put employees in a safety frame of mind.

Example 2

Equipment Maintenance: United States Navy

Need:

The context for the introduction of this heuristic job aid was the need to reduce operating costs in Navy clubs, partly through regularly scheduled equipment maintenance. Workers charged with maintenance in Navy clubs did not know when to perform regular maintenance procedures. Most important, they did not have a clear picture of the importance of the task and did not realize that the lack of regular maintenance resulted in increased repair and maintenance costs.

At the time, Marianne Hoffman was Head of Training Development for the Navy Recreational Services Unit of the Naval Military Personnel Command. Hoffman found that the function of conducting routine mainte-

nance was spread across several jobs subject to high turnover. This fact meant that a lengthy explanation was required each time a new employee was assigned maintenance tasks. She established the need for an ongoing system to support club personnel who were responsible for maintenance procedures.

Development:

Hoffman worked with one Navy cost-control expert for two days to develop the job aid. The job aid was tested first with individuals and then with groups during three cost-control course pilots.

The job aid is presented through step, checklist, and decision-table formats. It is delivered through print on card stock. Figure 9.2 shows the job aid that Hoffman developed.

Delivery and Maintenance:

This coaching/decision-making job aid was used to guide the training of employees of Navy clubs. It was one of eighteen job aids used in a cost-control course. During the course, personnel were required to demonstrate competence using the job aid. The trained personnel then returned to the field and either performed maintenance tasks themselves or trained others and served as resources when colleagues tried their hands at routine maintenance.

Hoffman explains that integration of the job aid was easy because the Navy regularly turns to job aids (called "gouges" by sailors) when a problem or unfamiliar task arises. This job aid was designed to be useful without training. To avoid the need for frequent revisions, the developer omitted references to specific pieces of equipment.

Impact:

At the time this job aid was developed, students in one of the modules in Hoffman's cost-control course tracked the results of the course. To her delight, students reported significant savings or cost avoidance as a result of using the course and the eighteen job aids.

Lessons Learned:

This is an example of a job aid that supports both classroom learning and job performance. During the

TO MANAGE EQUIPMENT MAINTENANCE

1. GATHER MANUFACTURER'S AND SAFETY INSTRUCTIONS.

2. PREPARE CHECKLIST FOR EACH ITEM TO BE MAINTAINED.

- What equipment is to be maintained (name, location)
- When each maintenance task should be done (how often)
- How each task should be done (step by step)
- What chemicals or tools are needed (brand names)

3. ASSIGN MAINTENANCE RESPONSIBILITIES

- Teach employee responsible how to do each task
- Test employee for competence in each task assigned

4. REVIEW RESULTS

- Judge maintenance from random inspections (see other side)
- Get equipment down time, repair costs from records

5. CHOOSE BEST ACTION IF DOWNTIME OR REPAIR COSTS ARE EXCESSIVE:

IF	AND	AND	THEN DO
Due to Maintenance and/or your random inspections	→	Plan is based on manufacturer's and safety requirements.	Schedule maintenance or inspections for off-hours when equipment is not in use.
	→	Plan is not based on manufacturer's and safety requirements.	Revise plan to meet manufacturer's and safety requirements.
Due to breakdowns or failing outside inspections	Employees are following plan.	Plan is not based on manufacturer's and safety requirements.	Revise plan to follow manufacturer's and safety requirements.
		Plan is based on manufacturer's and safety requirements.	Recommend replacement of equipment.
	Employees are not following plan.	→	Retrain employees or re-assign maintenance tasks.

Figure 9.2. Combination Job Aid for Equipment Maintenance, Side 1

TO MAKE A RANDOM INSPECTION

CHECK CLEANLINESS

- ■ Odor?
- ■ Dirt or dust?
- ■ Spots, stains?
- ■ Gummy, greasy, gritty surfaces?

CHECK WIRING

- ■ Frayed, kinked, tangled cords/wires?
- ■ Loose sockets/plugs?
- ■ Electrical grounding not intact?
- ■ Moisture nearby?

CHECK PLUMBING/PIPING

- ■ Visible moisture?
- ■ Stains, drip marks?
- ■ Tangling, kinking (flexible tubing)?
- ■ Deterioration (rigid piping or flexible tubing)?
- ■ Drains unclean, smelly?

CHECK HEATING EQUIPMENT

- ■ Burners, coils crusted/greasy?
- ■ Buildup on heat sensors?
- ■ Thermostat inaccurate?
- ■ Use also Wiring, Plumbing, Gasket checklists.

CHECK COOLING EQUIPMENT

- ■ Dust on coils?
- ■ Mineral buildup?
- ■ Frost buildup?
- ■ Thermostat inaccurate?
- ■ Use also Wiring, Plumbing, Gasket checklists.

CHECK DISPENSERS

- ■ Buildup around nozzle?
- ■ Mixtures out of balance?
- ■ Amount dispensed incorrect?
- ■ Dripping nozzles?
- ■ CO_2 pressures incorrect?
- ■ Temperature of product incorrect?
- ■ Use also Wiring, Piping checklists.

CHECK SMALL APPLIANCES

- ■ Housing, parts dirty/worn?
- ■ Visible oil/moisture on housing?
- ■ "Funny" noise when running?
- ■ "Walking" when running?
- ■ Use also Wiring checklist.

CHECK SCALES

- ■ Weights incorrect?
- ■ Zero not showing when empty?
- ■ Not level?
- ■ Platform/pointer bent?

**IF YOU GET ANY YES ANSWERS,
SEE IF ROUTINE MAINTENANCE WAS DONE AS YOU PLANNED.**

**WHETHER YOU GET YES OR NO ANSWERS,
SEE IF DOWN TIME OR REPAIR COSTS FOR ANY EQUIPMENT ARE TOO HIGH.**

**IF DOWN TIME OR REPAIR COSTS ARE TOO HIGH,
SELECT THE BEST ACTION FROM THE TABLE IN NUMBER 5 ON THE OTHER SIDE.**

**Figure 9.2 (continued). Combination Job Aid for
Equipment Maintenance, Side 2**

course it served as an organizer; later it became a reminder for infrequently performed tasks. Laminating the job aid would have enhanced its use in the working environment. Although the job aid was distributed to the sailors and was able to stand alone in most cases, special cases arose in which the user needed additional information. In these cases, the "expert" was available. In addition, the trained person was responsible for ensuring that job aids were posted and available.

Hoffman attributed the success of this job aid in large part to collaboration with cost-control expert, James P. Astrauckas. Astrauckas provided in-depth knowledge of club maintenance, allowing Hoffman to concentrate on how to construct and deliver the job aid.

Example 3

Performance Management Checklist: Sharp HealthCare

Need:

A job aid is part of Sharp HealthCare's new performance-management course for 250 to 300 managers at hospitals and clinics throughout the county of San Diego, California. The purpose of the course is to launch and to maintain a new performance-management system that requires managers, with the input of staff, to develop job descriptions with measurable criteria. Ongoing performance review then is based on these criteria. Managers are required to communicate specific performance expectations and ratings to all employees. For example, if a score of "2" is acceptable performance within the customer-service category, the employee is informed that in order to receive a "2," he or she must receive between two and five positive customer-comment cards in a calendar quarter. In addition, throughout the year, the manager must assist, observe, measure, and document employee performance. Then the manager is expected to reassess and revise standards to suit the changing requirements and realities of the job.

Sharp HealthCare's Karen Morse worked with Audrey Bloom, an external consultant, to build a course that prepared managers to use the new perfor-

mance-management system. In addition, they developed an extensive series of job aids to capture the essence of the course and to enable managers to have ongoing review and quick reference once they had returned to their jobs.

Development:

This is a good example of a job aid that stretches the traditional applications of job aids by providing access to key information and by coaching managers in their approaches to this new process. Bloom reports spending three to five hours on this job aid, not including the time allocated to data collection and task analysis. A desktop publisher spent approximately two hours formatting the job aid.

The job aid has two parts, both of which use a checklist format. Part A lists key ideas related to "Ongoing Performance-Management Activities"; Part B provides information used before, during, and after the performance-evaluation meeting. The job aid is printed on a double-sized sheet of paper and can be copied on a standard copying machine. Figure 9.3 (pages 150-153) shows the job aid that Karen Morse and Audrey Bloom developed.

Delivery and Maintenance:

This coaching job aid was given to managers during a performance-management course or was mailed through internal mail. The job aid is contained as an appendix to the seventy-page "Sharp HealthCare 1991 Performance Management System." Managers are strongly encouraged to attend the training at least once and then to return for a refresher every two years.

These heuristic aids are used as content outlines during classes. Instructors display the job aids as overhead transparencies throughout the course in order to summarize points and to draw attention to the job aids in the manual. After training, in the normal course of work, if managers request assistance with specific topics related to performance management, the human-resources function at Sharp uses job aids to provide appropriate coaching.

This job aid was not designed to stand alone. Before managers are encouraged to rely on the job aid, they are expected to understand the human dynamics involved in performance management and to possess the technical skills inherent in writing performance evaluations and supervising criteria-based jobs.

Performance systems are not static entities. Every October Sharp uses a committee of managers and employees to review and to recommend changes to the performance-management system, manual, course, course materials, and job aids. The review date is printed on each manual so that managers know to seek out and to use the most recent version. In addition, the management-development staff may recommend and implement changes at any time throughout the year.

Impact:

The job aid was designed to summarize information delivered in the course and to provide managers with exposure to perspectives about performance management. It achieves these purposes. In addition, the job aid provides a firm foundation for teaching segments of the performance-management system. The job aid is well suited as an overhead transparency, thereby limiting the need for extensive development of course materials.

Lessons Learned:

Job aids are a good way to make courses more flexible and easier to update. By including job aids as the appendix to the performance-management manual, management can change or add to the course simply by adding or changing a job aid. In addition, the management-development staff can be sure that managers always have the newest version of the job aids. Bloom was glad that she used a simple and accessible desktop-publishing system to produce the aids. A final benefit of the heuristic job aid is that managers are provided with an overview of the entire process and with a mental set for engaging in what can be a troubling and ambiguous part of their responsibilities. When asked what she would have done differently, Bloom responded, "I would have added even more job aids."

Ongoing Performance-Management Activities

Communicate

Performance expectations:

- In depth with new employees
- Clarify continually, as necessary

Provide

Assistance and support:

- Deliver positive as well as constructive feedback
- Relate feedback to expectations described in the standards
- Coaching and counseling as necessary

**Observe
Measure
Document**

Employee performance, by:

- Observing or seeking observations of others on performance relative to the mutually agreed-on standards contained in the job description
- Documenting performance using meeting notes and minutes, notes of appreciation, complaints; reports and feedback from the employee's co-workers and other managers

**Reassess and
Revise Standards**

As appropriate to changing job responsibilities and assignments

Avoid

Performance evaluation pitfalls:

- Treating performance evaluation as an event rather than a process
- Evaluating *personality* traits rather than performance *behaviors*
- Relying on memory for examples of performance
- Overattention to some aspects of job performance out of proportion to the weight assigned to the standard

Figure 9.3. Checklist Job Aid for Performance-Management Activities

Preparing for the
Performance-Appraisal Meeting

**Approximately
Four Weeks
Before Meeting**

Provide the employee with:

- A copy of his/her position description
- The "Questions for Self-Appraisal" work sheet
- A copy of the booklet *Staff Performance Appraisal and Merit Increase Guide* (1991)

Remind the employee to return his or her "Questions for Self-Appraisal" notes within two weeks.

Remind the employee that performance feedback will also be collected from:

- Co-workers
- Other managers for whom he or she has worked

Seek input from other staff and managers about the employee's performance.

**Approximately
One-Two Weeks
Before Meeting**

Review the employee's position description.

Organize and review documentation (including the employee's self-appraisal notes). Review goals and expectations discussed and agreed to at the previous performance-appraisal meeting. Identify specific performance examples to support the evaluation.

Schedule a convenient time/place for a 45- to 60-minute meeting.

Meet with employee's lead, or direct report if applicable, to collect additional input.

Complete the Staff Performance Appraisal form:

- link (+) and (-) performance examples to standards
- record rating on each standard (1, 2, 3, or 4)
- at a minimum, write comments on those standards receiving a score of "1" (Does Not Meet) or "4" (Consistently Exceeds); and other standards as appropriate
- multiply rating (x) percentage weight for each standard
- determine overall point score
- calculate merit increase using *current* schedule

Summarize comments and prepare notes on a development plan.

**Figure 9.3 (continued). Checklist Job Aid
for Performance-Management Activities**

Conducting the Meeting

Bring

Be sure to have the following:
- A copy of the position description
- A copy of the Sharp HealthCare Mission and Values
- The performance appraisal form with all sections completed (except the "Employee Comments" section)
- Supporting documentation
- A copy of last year's performance appraisal

Review

The appraisal process/definitions with the employee. If necessary, explain:
- Standards (why used/how they benefit employee)
- Weights
- 1 - 2 - 3 - 4 point rating system
- How the overall rating serves as the basis for a merit increase

Communicate

The employee's value to the department/organization, and the value of his/her position.

Relate

The Mission and Values to the employee's performance standards, and actual performance.

Communicate

Performance Feedback:
- Compare actual performance to performance standards; cite observations and examples.
- Discuss each standard, at least briefly. Review the rating assigned to each standard.
- Comment on improvements in performance.
- Ask employee how he/she will work to raise any "1" ratings (if applicable).

Summarize

The discussion, convey overall rating.

Discuss

Merit increase, if applicable. Negotiate/record new goals.

Ask

Employee for feedback on weights and standards; draft revised standards if necessary.

Ask

For feedback on your own performance/how might you assist and support employee.

Allow

Time for employee to talk about personal issues or concerns, ideas, etc. Use active listening.

Figure 9.3 (continued). Checklist Job Aid for Performance-Management Activities

---

Follow-up Activities

Ask yourself: How did I handle the discussion?

- What did I do well?
- What surprised me about the meeting, and why?
- Was I prepared for the employee's questions?
- What could I have done better?
- What did I learn about this employee and the position?
- What did I learn about myself and my role as manager and leader?

Follow-up with employee as agreed during meeting. Continue to touch base with the employee on the progress of his/her development plan.

Complete and send an Employee-Status Change Form or Personnel Action Document to Human Resources.

**Figure 9.3 (continued). Checklist Job Aid
for Performance-Management Activities**

Example 4   *20 Things You Can Do Within 99 Seconds
to Improve Your Negotiations:
The Pacific Group*

Need:

This job aid was developed in response to a personal realization and a common professional need. While doing a personal inventory of strengths and weaknesses, Sam Shmikler, President of The Pacific Group, recognized that negotiating skills are an important competency for which he and most of the people with whom he worked had received no formal training.

In response to this, he decided to create a course to assist The Pacific Group's own staff and to use as a commercial offering available for delivery to training managers from other companies. The course's goal is simple—to improve a professional's negotiating skills.

The Pacific Group reviewed the literature and communicated with other performance technologists about underutilized or troublesome aspects of negotiation. Shmikler noted the importance of a certain kind of mind-set about negotiating. This led Shmikler to add a job aid to the negotiating course, one that would be used on the job, just before, during, and after a person confronts the need to negotiate effectively.

Development:

This is an example of a job aid that is designed to coach performance prior to, during, and immediately after a negotiating session. To develop this job aid, Shmikler drew from personal experience, the experiences of colleagues, and texts such as The Art of Negotiating, You Can Negotiate Anything, *and* Getting to Yes. *This job aid was developed in about fifteen hours, including research and numerous rounds of revisions.*

This coaching job aid relies on a checklist format and is delivered through print on laminated card stock. It is delivered in two forms: an 8½" x 11" size that is bound in a three-ring binder for use during the course and a 4" x 7" size that managers can keep in their planning calendars. Figure 9.4 shows the job aid that Shmikler developed.

Delivery and Maintenance:

The job aid is delivered as part of a course. Shmikler uses the job aid to pull all the information together after it has been taught. The job aid links information and examples from the course in a series of concisely stated points. During the course, Shmikler encourages participants to use the job aid to complete case exercises. After the course, he believes that someone can use it to get into the proper frame of mind for negotiating and to review ways to be successful. Although the job aid was not designed to stand alone without the course, Shmikler supposes that an experienced person would find it a useful tool.

Shmikler has revised the job aid ten times since its origin. He has no set schedule for updates but incorporates comments from course participants and colleagues periodically.

Impact:

Both versions of the job aid served their purposes: providing clear representations of the factors to consider when preparing for, conducting, and reflecting on a negotiation. Shmikler judges the success of the job aid through the increasing number of course participants who encourage others in their organizations to attend the negotiation class and who request copies of the job aid.

20 Things You Can Do Within 99 Seconds to Improve Your Negotiations

Sam Shmikler

The Pacific Group
13101 Washington Blvd.
Los Angeles, CA 90066
213/306-1779
FAX 213/827-5141

1. Communicate your interest in reaching and implementing a solution.

2. Confirm the perceived status in the room by checking seating.

3. Trace eye-contact patterns.

4. Suggest that both parties face the problem together rather than face each other.

5. Determine the easy ones from the tough ones to solve.

6. Look for signals of common interests: kids, pets, fishing, NSPI.

7. Restate one of the objectives/outcomes of your negotiation.

8. Tell yourself what happens if you don't ever get an agreement—it's sobering!

9. Mentally rehearse everyone's name in the room (if you don't know people) so you can call everyone by name.

10. Listen to the tone of the room. When someone's vocal tone/volume shifts, who follows immediately.

11. Remember to repeat what you heard the others say, BEFORE YOU OFFER YOUR REACTION.

12. Privately ask yourself, "What am I building right now that will lead to a long term business relationship?"

13. Look forward, not backward.

14. Write out the four obstacles to brainstorming on your note pad:

    - Premature judgment
    - Searching for a single answer
    - Assumption of a fixed pie
    - Thinking that "solving their problem is their problem," when in fact, it's yours too.

15. Balance broad brainstorming ideas with very specific ideas.

16. When confronted with someone who breaks the rules—restate your interpretation of the rules. Don't try to break the person.

17. Remember the entire process is the "cop," not just you as an individual.

18. When you hear an attack on you, try to hear it as an attack on the problem.

19. Operate from the process side.

20. Never let 'em see you sweat!

Figure 9.4. Checklist Job Aid for Negotiation Skills

Shmikler uses the job aid himself and often distributes it to members of a negotiating team. He finds that it not only improves his ability to negotiate, but also improves the approach of others involved in the process.

Lessons Learned:

This job aid illustrates a job aid that coaches performance before, during, and after the challenge. Shmikler's only suggestion for change in the heuristic aid would be to reorder the guidelines so that they match the chronological progression of most negotiating sessions. The job aid really works. It helps course participants to work through case studies during the course and provides a means for HRD professionals to continue to inventory and to improve their negotiating skills.

Review of Examples

This chapter illustrated how four professionals used job aids to solve different, but typical, problems.

Bob Hobbs of GTE provided a job aid to ensure safety consciousness on the part of employees who dig trenches. Hobbs provided job aids that offered ready access to the overall process for properly digging excavations and trenches. In addition, his job aid directs employee attention to the aspects of the job with the greatest safety hazards. Because many crews do this work, Bob distributed the job aid first to supervisors, who then distributed it to their employees. The pocket job aids are part of a campaign to make supervisors and employees responsible for their own safety.

Marianne Hoffman developed an heuristic job aid for Navy club employees to use when planning for and conducting regular equipment maintenance. This job aid resulted in lowered or avoided costs through scheduling and performing proper equipment maintenance.

Karen Morse and Audrey Bloom produced a coaching job aid for a new performance-management system. Sharp Health-Care, an organization that emphasizes quality and employee standards, turned to job aids to help managers to handle a major organizational shift to a criteria-based performance-management system. The job aid supports managers in a potentially stressful process and in the individual events that it comprises.

Sam Shmikler developed job aids to help professionals who are involved in negotiations. This job aid summarizes key points covered in his workshop, supports participants as they complete case studies during the class, and serves as a planning and self-evaluation tool once the professionals have returned to their jobs.

Review of Chapter 9

Job Aids for Decision Making and Coaching Are Needed When:

- There is a need to influence perspective;
- The user needs to know how to approach a problem;
- There is room for ongoing improvement;
- The performance is infrequent;
- The employees who do the job change frequently;
- The consequences of error are high;
- The situation is complex;
- The job or organization is changing and employees need to do their work differently;
- There is no need to memorize information; or
- There are insufficient resources for training large numbers of employees.

Job Aids for Decision Making and Coaching Use These Formats:

- Checklist;
- Array;
- Decision table; or
- Flow chart.

Job Aids for Decision Making and Coaching Use These Media and Packaging:

- Laminated paper with color highlights;
- Paper bound in a three-ring binder;
- Double sheets of paper, bound in a three-ring binder;
- Laminated paper, bound in a three-ring binder;
- Laminated card stock, packaged with the training materials and packaged separately to fit in a weekly planner;

- Poster sized;
- On-line; or
- Audio.

Job Aids for Decision Making and Coaching Use These Mechanisms for Delivery and Maintenance:

- Used during training and used to support on-the-job performance;
- Stand alone, posted at work site;
- As structure for the training course;
- As support for training activities;
- Automated help screens or imbedded prompts; and
- Recorded on audiotapes to review strategies or factors to consider.

Job Aids for Decision Making and Coaching Have These Impacts:

- Improved performance;
- Quicker dissemination of complex information;
- Increased profit and/or savings;
- Fewer accidents;
- Fewer errors;
- Increased confidence;
- Better collaborative habits between developers and line employees; and
- Improved standards for performance-management systems.

Job Aids for Decision Making and Coaching Result in These Lessons Learned:

- Consider the whole job and then make decisions about what job aids are needed;
- Collaborate with line employees and field test the job aid early in the development stage;
- Use combinations of formats to help employees visualize complex processes;
- Include job aids as part of training; and
- Train a cadre of job-aid experts to serve as resources back at the work site.

Preview of Chapter 10

Chapter 10 focuses on the future of organizations. It examines how computer technologies, changes in organizations, demographics, and greater emphasis on performance and accomplishments are expanding and shaping the future of job aids.

References

Cohen, H. (1983). *You can negotiate anything.* New York: Bantam.

Fisher, R., and Ury, W.L. (1983). *Getting to yes: Negotiating agreement without giving in.* New York: Penguin.

Nierenberg, G.I. (1984). *The art of negotiating.* New York: Pocket Books.

Part Four

Trends in Job Aids

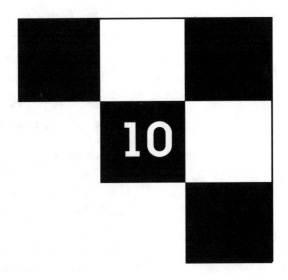

Into the Future:
Trends in Organizations

My-Lan, a plant manager, wants employees to receive training at their work stations, on the floor of the manufacturing facility. She is dissatisfied with sending people away for training and has some doubts about whether or not that training affects their work.

Peg directs a new group of course developers and documentation specialists for a large computer company. She is delighted about the reorganization that has joined these two kinds of professionals and is looking for ways to use their combined skills and perspectives.

Jeff, a sales trainer, is responsible for ensuring that all his company's reference books on products, prices, and peripherals are up-to-date. He thinks there must be a better approach than his current way of doing it.

Chapter 10 examines the influential forces in organizations. The following forces are influencing current job aids and the aids emerging for the future:

- Organizational shifts;
- Demographic shifts;
- Cost pressures;
- Integrated work and performance systems;
- Emphasis on performance and accomplishment; and
- Computer technologies.

Job aids, conceptualized as they are in this handbook, will continue to be a dominant factor in the organization of the 1990s and on into the next century. The HRD professional is confronting new pressures and possibilities. On the one hand, organizations face major social and economic pressures. On the other hand, computer technology is enabling explosive new capabilities across the organization, including capabilities in the development and delivery of job aids.

Organizational Shifts

Major and lasting organizational trends can be summed up in three phrases: responsiveness to customers and markets, a quality orientation, and a reduced number of middle managers. How do these three trends affect job aids?

Responsiveness to customers and markets. This first trend drives information and services away from central headquarters and to the markets. Customers want what they want when they want it. Job aids, especially automated informational and coaching aids, will be enable organizations to meet customer demands by responding to the needs of dispersed populations for data bases that capture and convey volatile subject matter.

A quality orientation. The "quality movement" of the late 1980s is becoming an integral part of the American organizational psyche. Witness the hold that the much-touted Malcolm Baldrige Award has on corporations. Concepts central to the quality movement are a wider dissemination of information throughout the organization and the increased participation in decision making that emerges from the enhanced flow of information. Job aids will be major players in expanding access to information.

A reduced number of middle managers. The third organizational trend is often expressed as movement toward flatter organizations, with fewer managers to ensure productivity. Job aids will be expected to contribute to filling this supervisory void. As surrogates for experience and expertise, job aids can be used to prompt and to guide employees and to enlighten their performance.

Demographic Shifts

By the twenty-first century, white males will represent a smaller percentage of the work force than they do now. The number of workers between the ages of sixteen and twenty-four also will decrease; a 25-percent reduction in the availability of youth for entry-level positions is estimated. The work force is becoming increasingly female, minority, limited in English proficiency, and elderly.

The scenarios that result from these demographic shifts depend in large part on the success of the public schools in preparing youth for life and work. The scenarios also depend, at least in part, on the kind of child care and medical support that individual organizations and the Federal government will elect to provide to working mothers and graying employees.

Most futurists are not optimistic. They express concern about weak skills—especially in science and math—and inadequate English proficiency. In the United States, the dropout and adult illiteracy rates are much greater than in Japan or in Europe. American organizations are increasingly pressured to solve the problems that kindergarten through twelfth-grade education and government agencies have failed to address. This translates into ongoing and growing investments in training and development.

Will the organizations of the future make that commitment? If the past is any indicator, they probably will not. Carnevale and Gainer (1989) judge that American organizations currently offer training and development opportunities to only 35 percent of their employees, and report that minorities are least likely to be recipients of such opportunities. Although they urge an expenditure of 4 percent of payroll on training and development, they estimate that organizations in the United States currently spend only 1.4 percent.

If underskilled workers enter organizations that are reluctant to expend resources to boost skills, then job aids will grow in importance. The power of job aids comes from their potential for providing information, specifying detailed procedures, and coaching performance—within the work context and at prices organizations perceive as affordable.

Cost Pressures

The cost of training and development is enormous, with estimates approaching $100 billion per year in the United States alone. One example makes the point. A few years ago, IBM estimated that it invested $900 million annually in education and training; the current estimate is $1.25 billion dollars per year. These statistics represent just one company.

Do organizations view the money they spend on training as a cost, or is this money perceived as an investment in people and programs? Unfortunately, most organizations see only cost, because the return on investment associated with training remains murky.

The future will see increased cost consciousness and more pressure for tangible results and proven links to the challenges that people face at work. Job aids, with their ability to diminish costs and to provide ongoing support for people on the job, will be assigned expanded roles.

Integrated Work and Performance Systems

The traditional role of training is often perceived as distinct from the world of work. Corporations support education and training centers, where individuals go to remove themselves from the flotsam and jetsam of their daily positions. Classes usually take people away from their work sites. Instructors describe their roles as building skills in preparation for work, but engineers create systems and programs in virtual isolation from training and documentation professionals.

Currently comments such as the following can be heard:

"In three weeks we'll be rolling out that new software package, and we need you to get people ready to use it. Here's the code, as it stands now. Don't forget to put together a snappy manual."

"I know I told you that it would be ready for the line by the first of the year, but the schedule has slipped. You'll just have to bring the workers back through training again, closer to the start date, so they'll remember how to work it. I know they've forgotten by now."

"You've had the managers out here for sessions on this performance-appraisal system before, but it doesn't seem to be working. The appraisals are still late, missing, or useless. Let's cycle them through again. Maybe we should lengthen the training sessions?"

These comments reflect the peculiar and ancillary role of training in most organizations. The 1990s are giving birth to a new and evolving mind-set. In the future, the distinctions among systems, training, and documentation and the distinctions between work and training will blur. It will be an era of new forms of user interface, professional development, and support systems. As Carr (1990) points out:

> It [the system] trains as a normal part of its operation. It trains the user to operate it effectively. More importantly, when certain expertise is necessary for the user to do his job, it helps him develop the expertise. It even keeps track of how expert he becomes, so it can interact with him at the appropriate level.... If the expertise is extrinsic to the job,...it either talks the user through the process or simply asks for the necessary information. In short, the system acts as an incredibly powerful job aid. (p. 19)

What training and development professionals know about assessing learners, building responsive interventions, structuring information, presenting feedback, providing help, coaching performance, and tailoring systems to people will remain essential to the organization. The innovative notion is that in the future training and development concepts—and job aids—will insinuate themselves earlier, continually, and seamlessly into the flow of work and the systems that support it.

Emphasis on Performance and Accomplishment

Why do training and development professionals exist within organizations? The following are wrong answers: to develop courses, to create computer-based training, to write job aids, to administer training programs, to evaluate courses, or to conduct needs assessments. These answers are wrong because they describe some of the things that HRD professionals do, not why they do these things.

There is only one correct answer: Training and development professionals exist to help an organization—or an individual—to do and to be its very best.

Although strategies and interventions vary from situation to situation, the broad mission does not vary. The orientation of human resources inevitably must shift to focus on the organizational goal and on helping employees contribute to that goal rather than on courses, student days, and training products. The new perspective inevitably leads to an increased reliance on job aids.

Puterbaugh, Rosenberg, and Sofman (1989), all of AT&T, likened this time in the history of human resource development to what the railroads confronted in the 1930s. At that time, railroad management could have acquired fledgling airlines for a song. They did not do so, however, because railroad leaders saw themselves in the railroad business rather than in the airplane business. Had they broadened their vision of what they were and defined themselves to be in the transportation world, their futures would have been much, much brighter.

Gilbert (1978) points out that training professionals must concentrate on and contribute to performance and accomplishment. This puts the training and development function where it ought to be, right in the middle of every enterprise, whether sales, safety, maintenance, mining, social services, prisons, schooling, food, space, health, or computers.

Computer Technologies

Computer technology is now readily accessible to the instructional designer and to the human resources manager. Hardware grows increasingly powerful and readily can be networked with mini- and mainframe computers. Software-development tools can now be used by the average person.

Gery (1989) wrote the following:

> Historically, the biggest issues in electronic performance support have been technical: limited, slow, inadequate hardware and lack of software. As with the telegraph and the steam engine, however, the technical problems have been overcome and we simply require the vision to actually implement it. It is now relatively simple to identify and acquire hardware and to buy development software. (p. 21)

It is impossible to overestimate the impact that decreased prices, increased speed, enhanced memory, and friendlier and more accessible systems will have on the future of job aids.

Conclusion

The situations faced by My-Lan, Peg, and Jeff reflect the trends described in this chapter.

My-Lan has broad responsibilities for manufacturing units. She is skeptical about the costs and benefits of removing people from their jobs so that they can travel to a training class. She cannot remember seeing any changes in her people as a result of the time spent off-site. Her concerns point to a growing role for job aids.

Peg thinks she has something unique in her organization. She plans to coordinate information and education efforts toward an appropriate mix of solutions to client problems. When queried, she expressed her opinion that there will be a shift toward the use of technology to deliver both information and training. She thinks that in some ways her organization is defining the future, through an integrated approach that has the designers of data bases, job aids, and training working side by side.

Jeff is frustrated with the labor-intensive process by which he mails updates to regional sales offices across the nation and then trusts that the information will find its way into thousands of reference books. He knows what goes on in the field. Salespeople and managers, although dependent on current data, often neglect maintenance of their reference materials. He is interested in expert systems, on-line help systems, and performance-support tools, the topics covered in Chapter 11.

Review of Chapter 10

Chapter 10 has examined the influential forces in organizations. The following forces influence current job aids and the aids emerging for the future:

Organizational shifts:

- Toward a more market-driven approach;
- Toward more of a quality orientation; and
- Toward flatter organizations.

Demographic shifts:

- More female, minority, and elderly employees;
- Fewer workers between the ages of sixteen and twenty-four entering the work force; and
- More pressure on organizations to build basic skills.

Cost pressures:

- Reluctance to compensate for weak schools and skills; and

■ Demand for proof of return on investment.

Integrated work and performance systems:

■ Blurring distinction between work and training;

■ Blurred distinctions among technological systems, documentation systems, and training; and

■ Early and ongoing involvement of human resources.

The emphasis on performance and accomplishment:

■ Focus on contributions to the organizational mission rather than on student days; and

■ Focus on contributions to the organizational mission rather than on any one intervention.

Computer technologies:

■ Cheaper, faster, quicker hardware;

■ More connections; and

■ Accessible and friendly software.

Preview of Chapter 11

Chapter 11 describes what will happen when the preceding factors come together in the future. It defines and provide examples of a technological future for job aids.

References

Carnevale, A.P., & Gainer, L.J. (1989). *The Learning Enterprise.* Alexandria, VA: American Society for Training and Development.

Carr, C. (1990). Designing systems for the 90's. *Performance Improvement Quarterly, 3*(1), 14-26.

Clancy, J.A. (1989) Training workers for the factory of the future. *Training and Development Journal, 43*(2), 46-49.

Gery, G.J. (1989). The quest for electronic performance support. *CBT Directions, 2*(7), 21-23.

Gilbert, T.F. (1978). *Human competence: Engineering worthy performance.* New York: McGraw-Hill.

Puterbaugh, G., Rosenberg, M., & Sofman, R. (1989). Performance support tools: A step beyond training. *Performance and Instruction, 28*(10). 1-5.

Rossett, A. (1990). Overcoming obstacles to needs assessment. *Training: The Magazine of Human Resources Development, 27*(3), 36-41.

Technology for Job Aids

Mack, delayed at Los Angeles International Airport after attending a conference on technology and training, is overheard saying, "Sure. Sure. Sure. A computer is the answer. Paper is going to disappear. No more bulky reference manuals. This I have to see."

Julie, a training manager for a large bank, attended the same conference. She, however, is eagerly creating a list of hardware and software vendors who can help move her organization toward on-line help and expert systems.

Deron, a course developer for a large telecommunications company, is at the airport too. Working at his lap-top computer and using special software known as a performance-support tool, he is generating practice and test items for a course he is writing.

Chapter 11 looks at the implications of technology for job aids by focusing on the following three different but related systems:

1. On-line help systems;
2. Expert systems; and
3. Performance-support systems or tools.

Introduction

On-line help, expert systems, and performance-support systems represent the present and the future. Although they play key roles in only a few corporations and agencies today, for most organizations the merger of technology and job aids presents an opportunity for the future.

As stated previously, job aids can be categorized in three ways: (1) job aids that inform; (2) job aids that prompt procedures; and (3) job aids that provide advice on perspectives and decisions. What technology promises, and in some cases now delivers, is the opportunity to enhance and to combine these purposes into a speedy and responsive package.

The future of job aids is increasingly wed to technology. This chapter describes and provides examples of this marriage, focusing on how these technologies can improve human performance rather than on how they work their wonders.

On-line Help Systems

On-line help systems are the most familiar technological job aid. In fact, on-line help systems represented the first wave of electronic job aids. Accessible at a computer work station and embedded in software, help systems provide "just-in-time" support to the worker when and where needed. For example, computer users who experience problems using a new piece of software can use the help key to display an array of help options. The user selects the help topic most likely to meet his or her needs. Figure 11.1 is an example of the help that is offered to a new user of Apple Computer's popular HyperCard program.

The following section reviews the kinds of assistance that a help system can currently provide and will provide in the future:

Command assistance: This is the familiar help line that is present at the bottom of the screen, available in a pull-down menu, or accessed by pressing a help key or a question mark (?) plus a command. The quality of this assistance is based on the designer's ability to anticipate the needs of the user and the user's awareness of the kind of help to seek.

Documentation: This is electronic access to the familiar hard-copy documentation. On the one hand, it is comprehensive; on the other hand, on-line documentation can be

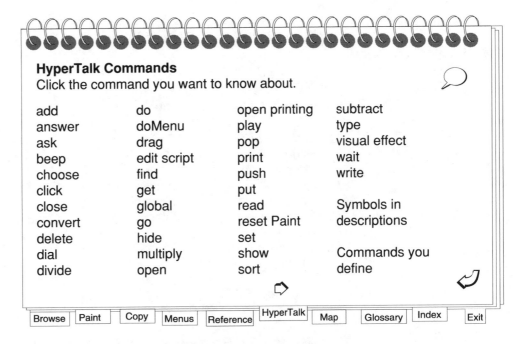

Figure 11.1. Array Job Aid for On-Line Help Systems

overwhelming because electronic page turning is even less palatable than plowing through thick manuals. Traditional on-line documentation is menu driven, with topics available through series of nested, potentially tedious, menus. Figures 11.2 and 11.3 from the HyperCard help program provide examples of two formats for menus, verbal and graphic.

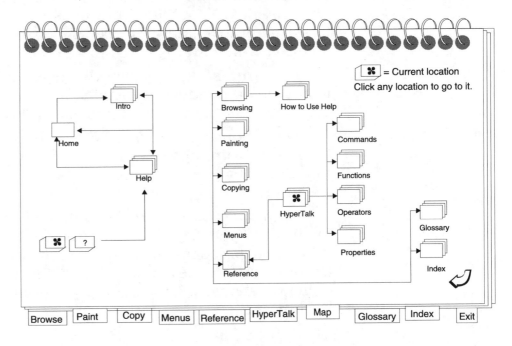

Figure 11.2. Graphic On-Line Help System Menu

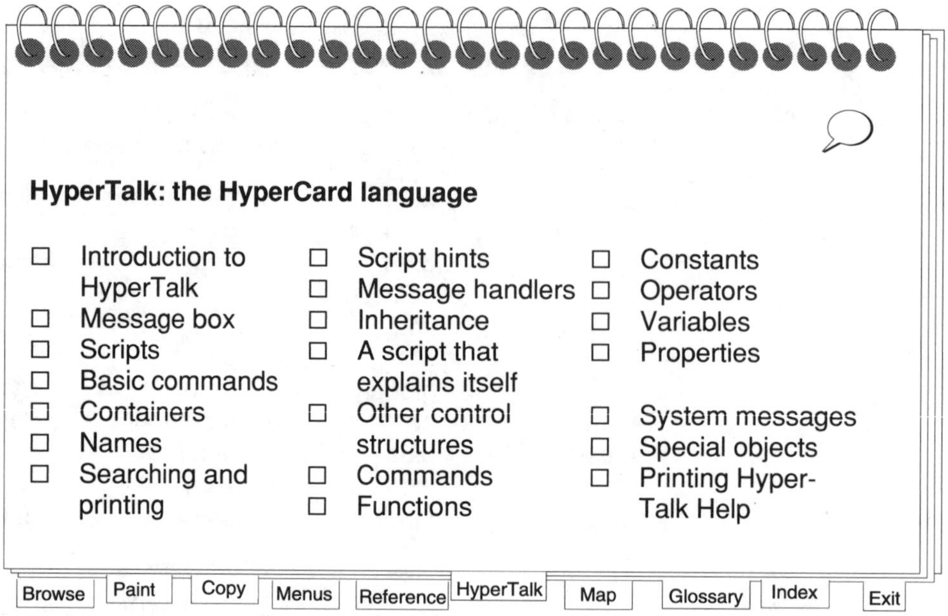

HyperTalk: the HyperCard language

- Introduction to HyperTalk
- Message box
- Scripts
- Basic commands
- Containers
- Names
- Searching and printing

- Script hints
- Message handlers
- Inheritance
- A script that explains itself
- Other control structures
- Commands
- Functions

- Constants
- Operators
- Variables
- Properties

- System messages
- Special objects
- Printing Hyper-Talk Help

`Browse` `Paint` `Copy` `Menus` `Reference` `HyperTalk` `Map` `Glossary` `Index` `Exit`

Figure 11.3. Verbal On-Line Help System Menu

Eventually, instantaneous access and browsing will be supported by natural-language searching. The user will type a phrase or name and immediately will be presented with all appropriate passages. Apple's HyperCard is a powerful example of this emergent tool. The example in Figure 11.4 is taken from an orientation program that was developed by Jeff Brechlin and Allison Rossett for Apple Computer, Inc. A user enters COMMAND-F or clicks the mouse on FIND, enters a natural-language choice, like "travel reimbursement" or "Sculley," and is swiftly taken to information on that subject.

Error assistance: When the user makes an error, the help system identifies it independently. At present, however, only a few on-line help systems offer this option.

Performance prompting: When the user makes an error, he or she is prompted as to what to do next. This anticipatory and diagnostic feature will be increasingly common in the future.

Learning opportunities: On-line help systems also can tutor users. Systems currently provide definitions, examples, drills, and practices to support individual growth. Dynamic learning experiences, though a highly desirable component of help systems, will be more a feature of the future than of the present.

**Figure 11.4. Access to Information
Through Natural-Language**

Current on-line help systems serve primarily as information and procedural job aids. Although these systems are usually associated with support for software and hardware, most of them fail to tailor responses to the user automatically, force the user to depart from the application at hand in order to consult the help system, and are what Cohill and Williges (1985, p. 335) call "essentially compressed versions of reference manuals."

Unfortunately, the problem with many help systems is that they rely on the user to know what is needed. Figures 11.1 through 11.3 are examples of this problem. The system provides definitions and procedural help only if the user can identify the problem.

As they evolve, on-line help systems will take better advantage of the computers in which they reside, becoming responsive, accessible, and personalized, more like the HyperCard orientation depicted in Figure 11.4. Help systems will be integrated into work and will include the use of split screens that enable help and work to occur simultaneously. A longer-term goal is to have systems that anticipate individual user problems and offer appropriate suggestions when needed. This example of system "intelligence" leads to a discussion of expert systems.

Expert systems, like on-line help systems, exist to support the user during work. Capitalizing on the powers of the computer, an expert system works in the role of adviser, in an aggressive coaching role, rather than as a passive compendium of information and procedures. Figure 11.5 presents commonalities and differences in help and expert systems.

As Feigenbaum, McCorduck, and Nii (1988) point out, expert systems are intellectual assistants. They are colleagues, servants, and advisers, not bosses. Although help systems are primarily involved in the introduction and use of hardware and software, expert systems can be applied to most challenges (for example, emergency medical dispatch, inventory control and equipment, arithmetic, and medical diagnosis).

When people use expert systems, they use the screen and keyboard to interface with the expert system software within the computer. That software is created in two ways. In systems built from scratch, professionals (sometimes called knowledge engineers) take the best thinking of one or several experts and collaborate with programmers to develop the

	On-Line Help Systems	Expert Systems
Roles:	To provide information	Invisible information
	To provide procedures	Invisible procedures
		To coach and to advise on actions and decisions
		To explain why
Uses:	Hardware and software systems	Every kind of problem
Sources:	Factual knowledge	Factual and heuristic knowledge
	Facts, procedures, accessible data	Facts, procedures, accessible data, and human expertise

**Figure 11.5. Comparison of On-Line Help
and Expert Systems as Job Aids**

code that expresses that human expertise. The alternative development method is reliance on expert system shells. These shells, described and reviewed in Paul Harmon's newsletter, *Intelligent Software Strategies*, are friendly programming structures into which nonprofessional programmers can readily plug new facts and heuristics.

An expert system can serve the following functions:

1. Through a question-and-answer process available on the computer screen, an expert system can serve as a coach to prompt and direct the user based on the facts of a particular situation.

2. Expert systems extend expertise by increasing the number of people in an organization who can handle a particular domain of problems. The expert system is expected to boost performance by suggesting questions, answers, actions, regulations, concerns, and eventualities to novices.

3. An expert system is a knowledgeable support system that is omnipresent. For example, Feigenbaum et al. (1988) described the office for Great Britain's retirement system; millions of citizens call, write, and wait for solutions to varied and complicated problems. To address problems with sluggish and inaccurate responses, Arthur Andersen, Inc., built an expert system to support office workers. It is always there, patient, accessible, and as accurate as the factual regulations and human expertise programmed into the system.

4. Expert systems support workers in ambiguous situations. Obviously, computers are extraordinary tools for "crunching numbers." Far more important to the training professional is their potential for helping employees to solve complex problems whose answers are ambiguous. Does the company need to order more supplies now or can the order wait? Which investment is best for a particular client? Which used car is best? How much of a loan can a particular person afford? What kind of medical tests should be done on a particular patient? The expert system answers these questions by making a recommendation or a range of recommendations, each of which is presented with a confidence rating. The options and strength of the recommendations are derived by summarizing experts' levels of certainty about a particular course of action applied to a given circumstance.

5. An expert system can explain why it is making a particular suggestion. As Welsh and Wilson (1987) point out, most expert systems provide a path for reviewing how the system has arrived at its recommendations. This powerful option makes overt the facts, heuristics, confidence ratings, and inferences that have influenced the suggestions. Examining the reasoning process of these programs is fascinating. In addition, this option reveals and models expert thinking for novices and provides enough information to enable a more experienced user to elect to by-pass the system's advice.

6. It presents itself to the user as a clear and friendly interface. Although a data base and complex rules govern expert system software, these components are invisible to the user unless sought. What the user experiences is a lean and interactive process of questions, answers, and suggestions. Lewis (1990), in an article in *The New York Times*, illustrates the possibilities of such a system. Lewis describes *Performance Mentor*, an IBM-compatible expert system from a Palo Alto company by the same name that helps managers to prepare for and to conduct performance reviews. A good example of a job aid that is an influence just prior to and during performance, this expert system advises managers on the conduct of this important interaction.

7. An expert system can be used as a diagnostic and prescriptive tool. The computer screen asks for information, the user inputs the information, and the screen displays recommendations.

Two examples are useful here. Some real estate salespeople rely on the computer to support interviews with prospective buyers. The sales associate, coached by the computer, asks questions about income, expenses, and housing requirements; the associate keys answers into an automated work sheet; the computer then offers recommendations regarding the individual's potential for home ownership, qualifications for a mortgage, and potential matches with listings from the housing stock. This produces a checklist of recommendations that the associate can use in communicating with the client.

A second example comes from the training world. Figures 11.6 and 11.7 are small pieces of a diagnostic expert system for the professional-development needs of instruc-

Scenario 1: THE DEVELOPMENT TEAM

It is late afternoon on a Friday, and you and four other members of the development team are gathered to talk about the project. This project has been a tough one involving a very busy co-developer, a new product under development, and a contractor with a history of tardiness and brilliance.

Which best describes your confidence and comfort as you work with your colleagues?

Figure 11.6. Diagnostic Expert System for Instructional Designers

COMMUNICATING and MANAGING

■ Secure win-win agreements between colleagues.

7	6	5	4	3	2	1
Very confident			Somewhat			Not at all

■ Ask people to report progress and problems and assign tasks based on this feedback.

7	6	5	4	3	2	1
Very confident			Somewhat			Not at all

Show Scenario

Figure 11.7. Diagnostic Expert System for Instructional Designers

tional designers. Designers confront scenarios from their own worlds and are expected to assess their confidence at handling the situations. The expert system then takes these self-assessments and tailors individualized professional-development opportunities.

Always there, always supportive, and always a patient booster of confidence, an expert system is like a child's invisible buddy. Like a child's buddy, however, most expert systems do not provide direct educational experiences. For the whole package—for a system of interconnected information, education, and advice—one must turn to performance-support tools.

By definition, performance-support tools (PSTs) embody all three kinds of job aids: they provide information, they support procedures, and they serve as coaches for decision making. In addition, PSTs tutor their users. Thus PSTs give the worker on-the-job electronic access to these three very desirable functions: information, education, and expert consultation.

PSTs are software packages that include and extend the capacities of on-line help and expert systems. Figure 11.8 depicts the relationship among on-line help, expert, and performance-support systems.

Puterbaugh, Rosenberg, and Sofman (1989, p. 2) define PSTs this way: "A performance-support tool is software designed to improve worker productivity by supplying immediate on-the-job access to integrated information, learning opportunities, and expert consultation—with scope and sequence controlled by the user."

Performance-support tools offer the following features:

1. Performance-support tools enable the user to gain access to large amounts of information. It is this feature that Puterbaugh, Rosenberg, and Sofman (1989) describe as interactive documentation. Moving beyond current help systems, PSTs provide a broad range of information types related to a particular domain and specific inquiry. Users can type natural-language

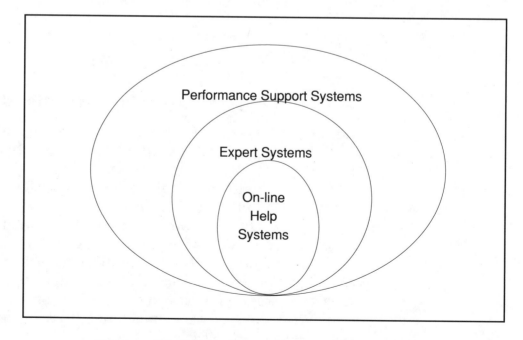

Figure 11.8. Performance-Support Tools

commands to browse through the available data via a function known as hypertext (for words and data) or hypermedia (when graphics are also accessible).

2. Performance-support tools include opportunities for learning. Puterbaugh, Rosenberg, and Sofman (1989) claim that this feature goes beyond the traditional drills and practices that are a part of on-line help systems to include dynamic examples, exercises, and simulations. Rosenberg recently demonstrated this feature in a PST designed to help training professionals to select appropriate solutions to problems and opportunities. The user is presented with a case; he or she then must make and justify decisions. The PST makes comments on these selections and eventually models an expert's approach to the case.

3. Performance-support tools are expert systems that provide advice and coaching. They ask questions, gather information, judge responses, and serve as consultants to users.

4. Performance-support tools offer a distinctive user interface. Through the interface, the three major functions of PSTs—information, education, and coaching—smoothly connect to one another and are simultaneously accessible to the user. With a few keystrokes, the user can move from a hypertext data base to a tutorial to a simulation, back to the data base, and then to a session with the adviser.

Two examples of PSTs are useful to present. The first comes from Jan Diamondstone, President of Interactive Design in Wilmington, Delaware. In a case study, Diamondstone (1988) describes a large manufacturing company that wanted to increase the productivity of its Employee Relations Department. Charged with carrying forward Equal Employment Opportunity (EEO) and Affirmative Action (AA) programs, the unit was eager to ensure that recruitment, hiring, retention, termination, internal progression, and career planning were in compliance with federal regulations as well as supportive of aggressive, internally defined goals. Regulations and advice were communicated by a group of internal experts to two hundred field sites. The goal of the project was to package the expertise of this consulting group so that it could be electronically accessible across a growing organization.

Diamondstone's company built a PST that does a lot for the user. It provides information on EEO/AA regulations and corporate policies. Users acquire the information they need through a hypertext key-word search. The PST also serves as a coach and confidence builder. Users are prompted through procedures and strategies appropriate to particular situations, whether they are handling complaints, responding to requests, or preventing problems. In addition, this PST offers learning opportunities by reflecting the way experts handle EEO/AA cases, by providing some simple computer-based training (CBT), and by directing users to instructional videotapes. Just as the expert from headquarters would have done, the program asks questions before providing answers. For example, it asks about the kind of charge, the alleged harm to the party, the law under which the charge was filed, and so on. Then the program coaches and advises the user.

A second PST example is the AT&T Training Test Consultant described by Puterbaugh, Rosenberg, and Sofman (1989) and produced for internal use only. This is the first in a series of PSTs designed to support AT&T training professionals; its goal is to help trainers to write better tests through access to these three tools:

1. *Infobase:* This interactive documentation provides information on selection and design of tests, test-item construction, test administration, test reliability and validity, and security. As in the EEO/AA example described previously, an Infobase user can use natural language to browse through this information at will.

2. *Tutor:* This is the learning-support component of the PST. It contains seven drill-and-practice tutorials on topics such as the following: criterion versus norm-referenced testing; constructing multiple-choice and matching items; and interpreting item-analysis data. Within the tutorial, the user can be whisked into Infobase with a single keystroke when the need arises.

3. *Advisor:* In this expert system, the user can receive advice on a testing issue or statistical assistance in evaluating the quality of a test. As is the case with Tutor and with the interface common to PSTs, Advisor allows immediate referral to Infobase without interrupting consultation with the expert system.

One benefit of this PST is illustrated in Figure 11.9. On the left is the stack of materials that AT&T course developers formerly used to support the development of tests. On the right, with the computer in the background, are the four diskettes that replace all the books, monographs, and manuals.

Performance-support tools represent the wave of the future. They combine and build on the capacities of help and

**Figure 11.9. Performance-Support Tool
for Test Development**

expert systems. Their strength lies in being omnipresent and multifaceted partners in the work place. The three functions of information, education, and consultation—combined with the advantages of access, connectedness, and speed—represent the very capabilities that employees and executives are increasingly seeking from training and development organizations.

Obstacles Confronting Technology and Job Aids

Automated job aids are so valuable to workers that one might wonder why they are not everywhere. There are several reasons:

- Empirical support for the assumption that automated job aids are better than manual job aids is lacking. Very little research exists on the topic of job aids; what little does exist primarily compares manual job aids with training.

- The people who are in positions to invest in technological job aids recognize that this generation of automated job aids is far from perfect. Many people who have used on-line help and expert systems report disappointing experiences. For example, on-line documentation is often awkward and tedious. When systems force users to depart from the task at hand, work is impeded. In fact, Morrison and Witmer (1984) found that print was a better, more portable job aid for equipment operation than computerized help systems, which force users to divide their attention.

■ In many organizations, the necessary technological delivery systems are not yet in place. Can computers communicate with each other within buildings and across miles? Do users have automated work stations?

■ People tend to resist what is new. The joining of technology and job aids is novel in many ways and introduces new technologies, new roles, and new organizational paradigms.

■ If manual job aids disrupt the traditional way that training departments receive their budgets, then the more expensive and extensive PSTs destroy conventional reimbursement systems. Because training departments traditionally have been paid on a per-trainee basis, PSTs require new ways of assessing contributions and reimbursing people for their efforts.

■ It is difficult to garner resources to support functions that cross over traditional department lines. If the ultimate goal of a PST is a tool that integrates information, education, and advice, then units representing training, methodology, planning, personnel, marketing, compensation, media services, documentation, and others must cooperate. The focus must be on performance and accomplishment, not on the conventional divisions and turf protection of disparate services.

Revisiting Mack, Julie, and Deron

Technology has immense potential for improving the way that job aids serve people and their organizations. To realize that potential requires what Gery (1989) and Puterbaugh, Rosenberg, and Sofman (1989) call a new mind-set, one that emphasizes the integration of work and performance support above any one type of solution.

Mack lacks that mind-set. Although he is committed to print-based job aids, he is skeptical about the benefits to be derived from automation and concerned about approaches that threaten his training classes. He needs to see examples that demonstrate comparative performance and cost benefits.

Julie, a manager for a large financial institution, should direct her enthusiasm toward organizational supports. Can she garner cross-departmental support? Are the necessary hardware delivery systems in place? Will upper-level executives work with her to find ways to reimburse her organization for automated performance support rather than for student days? Technological job aids cannot overcome organizational obstacles.

Deron has special responsibilities. He represents the first generation of users of performance-support tools. Deron must do more than use these tools; he must participate in substantive and irreverent analysis of their effectiveness. That empirical study is essential to building both the technology of automated job aids and the supportive mind-set for them.

Review of Chapter 11

On-line help systems have the following features:

■ Familiarity;

■ Just-in-time informational and procedural support;

■ Command assistance;

■ Extensive on-line documentation; and

■ Support for hardware and software installation and innovation.

Expert systems have the following features:

■ Capitalizing on the power of the computer;

■ Applying to many kinds of challenges;

■ Serving as coach through dialog with users;

■ Spreading expertise throughout the organization;

■ Supporting users in ambiguous situations; and

■ Serving as diagnostic and prescriptive tools.

Performance-support systems have the following features:

■ On-line access to information, education, and advice;

■ The ability to combine and expand on help and expert systems;

■ Immediate links between major tools; and

■ Dynamic learning opportunities.

Obstacles to using technology for job aids include the following:

■ Traditional organizations and mind-sets;

■ Departmental ownership and boundaries;

■ Challenges to typical reimbursement;

■ Resistance to innovation; and

■ Absence of empirical evidence and hardware support.

Preview of Chapter 12

Chapter 12 concludes this book. It summarizes where job aids have been and where they should be going.

References

Cohill, A.M., & Williges, R.C. (1985). Retrieval of help information for novice users of interactive computer systems. *Human Factors, 27*(3), 335-343.

Diamondstone, J. (1988). Beyond the bandaid: One company's use of CBT as a corporate strategy. *The CBT Digest, 2*(1), 4-9.

Feigenbaum, E., McCorduck, & Nii, H.P. (1988). *The Rise of the Expert Company.* New York: Times Books.

Gery, G.J. (1989). The quest for electronic performance support. *CBT Directions, 2*(7), 21-23.

Harmon, P. (1986). Expert systems, job aids, and the future of instructional technology. *Performance and Instruction, 25*(2), 26-28.

Harmon, P. (Ed.) *Intelligent Software Strategies.* Arlington, MA: Cutter Information Corporation.

Lewis, P.H. (1990, February 4). I'm sorry; my machine doesn't like your work. *The New York Times,* p. F27.

Morrison, J.E., & Witmer, B.G. (1984). A comparative evaluation of computer-based and print-based job performance aids. *Journal of Computer-Based Instruction, 10*(3 and 4), 73-75.

Puterbaugh, G., Rosenberg, M., & Sofman, R. (1989). Performance support tools: A step beyond training. *Performance and Instruction, 28*(10). 1-5.

Welsh, J.R., & Wilson, B.G. (1987). Expert system shells: Tools to aid human performance. *Journal of Instructional Development, 10*(2), 15-19

Conclusions About Job Aids

This chapter closes *A Handbook of Job Aids.* It covers two topics:

1. A description of the ten considerations that will increase the successful development and use of job aids; and
2. A recap of promises made at the beginning of the handbook.

Job-Aid Success

Chapter 12 summarizes the perspectives in this handbook that directly contribute to the successful use and development of job aids. Following are ten key considerations:

1. Good Job Aids Are Built on Good Needs Assessments

The handbook's message is not that job aids should be used at all times; the intent is to encourage their use when appropriate. Needs assessment provides information for making good decisions about when to employ job aids and about what needs to be done to support their introduction into the organization and the work site. Chapters 2, 3, and 6 make and develop this point.

2. Job Aids Must Be Introduced into the Environment Carefully and Systematically

Some job aids are best introduced in a formal class. Others can be given to employees by a supervisor, with encouraging words, commentaries, and demonstrations. Still others can find their way into the work flow simply by becoming available electronically. The important point is to consider carefully the users, the nature of the aid, and the history of job-aid use in the organization. Chapters 1, 3, 5, and 6 address this topic.

3. Job Aids Must Be Maintained and Revised

Some organizations have cultures that prize job aids, and they carefully attend to job-aid maintenance and updates. Most, however, do not. If job aids are to be useful, they must represent the products, procedures, data, and perspectives of today rather than those of yesterday. Chapters 6, 10, and 11 offer suggestions.

4. It Is Important To Be Aware of Three Kinds of Job Aids

Although traditional job aids provide information and prompt procedures, this handbook expands those domains to include aids that coach perspectives and decisions. Chapters 7, 8, and 9 provide examples and discussions that develop this concept. Swiftly changing organizations and expanding technology options press people to use job aids for all three types of situations. Chapters 4, 10, and 11 make and clarify these points.

5. Formats Should Match the Kind of Job Aid and the Work Site

Once it has been decided to develop a job aid, what options are there for formats? Chapter 5, 7, 8, and 9 present formats and examples for the development and delivery of job aids, each of which is linked to the different kinds of aids.

6. Developers Should Seek Out and Use the Job Aids That Develop Naturally Within the Organization

When she was a graduate student at San Diego State University, Nan Sterman (1988) conducted a small study of job aids in the work place. One of Sterman's most intriguing findings was that employees created job aids for themselves in the normal course of their work. Her study suggested that developers should build new job aids, where possible, on a foundation of the existing work—on the notes, notebooks, signs, and computer programs already available within the organization.

7. Job Aids Should Be Tested Before They Are Released into the Organization

One of the essential aspects of job aids is that they exist within the natural environment of the employee and the organization. For the most part, no one directly supervises their use. Thus, to be chosen by employees as productive parts of their work efforts, job aids must be congruent with the actual way people carry out their work. This will involve asking people in the organization to try out the job aid, using observations of their pilot attempts, and being willing to make changes in response to what is seen and heard. Chapter 6 covers this topic and provides checklists for ensuring the quality of job aids.

8. Job Aids Should Be Evaluated for Their Impacts on Individual, Unit, and Organizational Goals

Because job aids are natural to the flow of the work, their contributions are often ignored by the organization. Job aids become invisible even to the training professional who produced them as soon as the next project appears. It is important to reverse this trend by gathering data on cost and benefits and by making comparisons to other solutions. Chapters 2, 3, 6, and 10 discuss this topic.

9. Job Aids Should Be Promoted Within the Organization As Legitimate and Valued Performance Tools

Sterman's (1988) in-depth interviews with five professionals, each an experienced developer and user of job aids, unearthed some employee discomfort about relying on "cheat sheets," a term with obvious negative connotations. Her research suggested that employees and managers are not always comfortable with external supports for doing their jobs. Professionals must market the job-aid concept and prepare colleagues for a paradigm shift that diminishes traditional reliance on memory and training. Chapters 2, 3, and 10 deal with this issue.

10. Technology Presents New Opportunities for Both the Development and the Delivery of Job Aids

Job aids are now being developed by training professionals at computers, moving beyond the era of rulers and graphic artists. Even more intriguing is the potential delivery capacity offered by new technologies. Chapter 11 describes on-line help systems, expert systems, and performance-support systems as the emerging job aids of the 1990s and beyond. Chapter 10 discusses the societal and organizational trends that precipitated these changes.

The Goals of *A Handbook of Job Aids*

This handbook has two broad goals:

1. To be a useful tool by being a "job aid on job aids"; and

2. To establish new and expanded ways of defining job aids, approaches that broaden opportunities to employ job aids and that improve the quality of the aids that are developed.

Has the first goal been achieved? Is the handbook a useful tool? The promise that was made in the first chapter was that this handbook would itself serve as a job aid. If HRD professionals keep the handbook near their work stations, if they consult it as they conduct analyses with clients, if they turn to its examples to generate job-aid solutions of their own, and if they use it to evaluate plans and formats, then the first goal will have been achieved.

It is more difficult to assess fulfillment of the second goal. The following series of questions is addressed to the training and development professional:

- Can you define job aids?
- Are your definitions broader than those for traditional informational and procedural aids?
- Are you creating job aids that encourage approaches and perspectives?
- Are you developing checklists that serve as coaching guidelines?
- Are you using job aids in ways that are new for you and for your organization?
- Are you better able to use rational and compelling ideas and successful applications to sell job aids to clients?
- Are you and your clients asking hard questions about what must be retained in long-term memory and what can be supported by job aids?
- Are you creating job aids that you and your clients consider "better"?
- Are job aids used more?
- Is there more use of training to prepare employees to use job aids?
- Are there more requests from colleagues, clients, and customers for job aids?
- Are the distinctions between education and documentation in your organization being brought into question?

Ultimately, goal two has been achieved if professionals can answer many of these questions in the affirmative; if they are using the checklists sprinkled throughout the handbook to examine their own job aids; if they feel comfortable after that self-evaluation; and if they have identified, planned, and marketed new opportunities to boost performance with job aids without taking people away from the work site.

Conclusion

In the late 1970s, a colleague shared a cartoon that he had found in a magazine. He thought it was funny—and important. The cartoon was a series of panels that showed an individual walking carefully with a pencil, with the pencil cautiously pointed down. The heading and captioning suggested that this visual was used by a large company, one famed for its internal educational programs, as training for "How to Walk with a Pencil."

The creators of the cartoon did not know anything about job aids. What concerned them and inspired this cartoon was a supposed corporate view of the employee that analyzed jobs into tiny, mechanistic, and trivial components and then assumed that the American worker needed "training" to carry out even these small and mundane tasks.

This handbook contends that job aids have more to contribute than reminding people how to walk safely with a pencil. This handbook has put job aids forward as candidates for providing the following:

- Wider access to information by more people at more levels in the organization;
- Coaching for tricky or dangerous procedures and coaching for important and ambiguous approaches and perspectives;
- Opportunities to reconsider and to update jobs and the support systems that surround them;
- Cost-effective ways to boost performance;
- Vehicles for delivering information with a short shelf-life to the people who need to know;
- Patient and accessible support for new or under-skilled employees;
- Assistance for the individual employee who wants to be introspective, to conduct self-evaluation, and to carry out quality control; and
- Congruence with emerging societal, organizational, and technological trends.

For most training professionals, job aids rank in popularity with motherhood and apple pie. This handbook was created to contribute to the quality and diversity of job aids, thereby ensuring that they continue to earn enthusiasm and gratitude from these professionals and the organizations they serve.

Reference

Sterman, N. (1988). [Job aids in the work place.] Unpublished raw data.

Index

This book was edited and formatted using 386 PC platforms with 8MB RAM and high-resolution, dual-page monitors. The copy was produced using WordPerfect software; pages composed with Ventura Publisher software; illustrations produced in CorelDraw or hand-drawn. The text is set in twelve on fourteen Bookman Light and heads in Lubalin Bold. Proof copies were printed on a 400-dpi laser printer and final camera-ready output on a 1200-dpi laser imagesetter by Pfeiffer & Company.

Editor:

Marian K. Prokop

Editorial Assistance:

Jennifer O. Bryant and Carol Nolde

Cover, Interior Design, Art, Page Composition:

Kris Kircher